Tailoring
Ladies' Jackets

Step-by-Step Instructions

Mary Ellen Flury

Parker Publishing Company
Annapolis, Maryland

Published by:
Parker Publishing Company
2315 B Forest Drive, Suite 50
Annapolis, Maryland 21401

Library of Congress Catalog Card Number: 96-67001

ISBN: 1-883375-03-7

Designer: David Yao
Illustrator: John Payne
Photographer: Debbie Accame

Printed in the United States of America

This book is dedicated, with love, to my mother, Alice Warwick.
When I was a young girl, I learned how to sew by watching my mother
make many beautiful dresses, suits and coats for my sister and me.
This exposure to sewing at an early age, turned into my life-long career.

Table of Contents

Chapter 4
Sewing the Jacket   20

Chapter 5
Other Interfacing Options   74

Index

Acknowledgements

It is important for me to say thanks to the following individuals: to David Page Coffin for his editorial advice; to my sister, Patricia Moreland, who has given me more sewing challenges than any other person; to my good friends, Barbara Bowen and Leseal Kilcrease, for their encouragement; to Danny Moreland for his guidance throughout this project; to Sandra McCarter, for her computer expertise; to John Payne for the illustrations; to David Yao for the book design; and last, but not least, my mother, Alice Warwick, for teaching me how to sew.

Greetings!

Thanks for buying *Tailoring Ladies Jackets!* In this book you'll find directions that walk you step-by-step through the construction of almost any style of suit or separate jacket for women, using virtually any commercial pattern.

In fact, you can think of this book as an alternative to the instruction sheets that came with your pattern, referring to the instructions only for layout suggestions, and help with unusual designer details.

The construction processes covered in this book include:

- tailoring with fusibles
- tailoring with sew in canvas
- tailoring with fusibles and sew-in chest pads
- making and perfecting lapels and collars
- finishing necklines without lapels or collars
- making double welt pockets, with or without flaps
- making single welt pockets
- attaching patch pockets with no stitching showing
- making and setting in two-piece sleeves with vents

- making and setting in one piece sleeves without vents
- making bound buttonholes
- making buttonholes by machine
- using sleeve heads
- inserting shoulder pads
- making and attaching full linings.

My techniques for these details combine methods I learned from my mother, from my studies at The Catherine Olmstead School of Sewing and at The University of Maryland Home Economics Department (we were primarily taught the Bishop Method of clothing construction); from my over 40 years of professional experience in garment manufacturing, custom sewing, and alterations; and from teaching home sewers. During that time I've made well over 600 custom jackets for both men and women; altered, examined, puzzled over, and taken notes on countless manufactured jackets; visited a factory where I was able to carefully observe top-quality construction methods at work; and taught thousands of home sewers how to make top quality suits and jackets without spending either too much time or too much money.

Over and over, I've been impressed with the high-quality construction of men's jackets and suits, and been disappointed by the quality of similar garments made for women. And I've clearly seen the differences between how home sewers approach sewing challenges, and how factory sewers deal with them. In this book you'll get the best of both worlds: Menswear quality for women, and factory-level techniques that any reasonably confident sewer can use at home without a lot of industrial equipment or special skills. When you see the results that you can achieve following these methods, I'm sure you'll begin to love tailoring as much as I do. Thanks again, and have a wonderful time making YOUR ultimate jacket! ✑

Chapter 1

Getting Started

Most of these items are discussed in more detail immediately following this list, while others are discussed as they appear in the context of specific techniques.

Pattern

Select any commercial jacket pattern for your jacket or suit project. A few examples are (Figures 1.1a, 1.1b, 1.1c):

Figure 1.1a

Figure 1.1b

Figure 1.1c

Suiting fabric
Check yardage chart.

Lining fabric
Check yardage chart.

Fusible interfacing
(Check the interfacing options on page 78 for the supplies and techniques you'll need if you want to use primarily sew-in interfacings).
- Armo Weft — 1 1/2 to 2 yd.
- SofBrush or Whisper Weft — 1 1/2 to 2 yd.
- 100% Cotton, woven, fusible interfacing (Form-Flex) or other woven fusible — 1/4 yd.

Silesia (pocketing fabric)
- 3/8 yd.

Notions
- Thread — 3 spools
- Twill Tape (100% Cotton)
    1/4" wide — 1 yd.
    1/2" or 5/8" wide — 1 yd.
- Light-weight Muslin — Scraps
- Organza, or Seams Great
    3/8 yd. of organza, or 1 yd. of Seams Great
- Sleeve Wigan, 3" wide 1/2 yd.
- Shoulder Pads
    1/2" thick, covered, raglan pads,
- Sleeve Heads
    1 set, or poly batting scraps
- Scissors and shears
    Large (or rotary), for cutting
    Pinking, for cutting lining
    Small, for trimming and clipping
- Marking tools

Tailor's chalk
Sharp lead pencil
- Measuring tools
  Tape measure
  See-thru ruler
- Seam sealant (such as Fray Check).

Pressing tools

- Pressing cloth, seam roll, ham, clapper, point presser, and tailor's board with pads (Figures 1.2a, 1.2b, 1.2c, 1.2d).

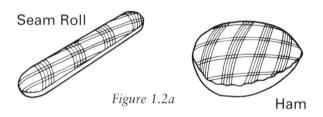

Seam Roll

Figure 1.2a

Ham

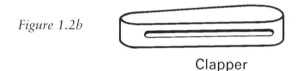

Figure 1.2b

Clapper

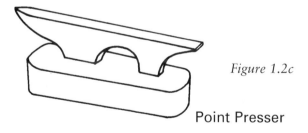

Figure 1.2c

Point Presser

Figure 1.2d

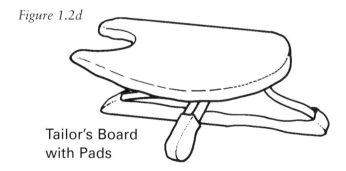

Tailor's Board
with Pads

Miscellaneous optional supplies

- Medium weight, sew-in Pellon
- Lightweight, non-woven, fusible interfacing (to reinforce pattern) — 3 yds.
- Cotton Batiste — 1/2 yd.
- Medium to heavyweight muslin for jacket fitting — 2 yds.
- Manilla folder, poster board, or template plastic and dressmaker's carbon tracing paper to make templates.

SUPPLIES IN DETAIL

Fabric selection

The fabrics suggested by the pattern company are helpful, but it's not necessary to limit your selection to just these. Many other fabrics on the market are as suitable. But do pay close attention to the "unsuitable" fabric list, because there's usually a good reason why they shouldn't be used. Suiting fabrics vary in fiber content, weight, thickness, draping, weaves, textures, etc., as well as in color, so it's important to handle the fabric to check the weight and feel before you decide to purchase it. I prefer natural fibers such as wools, cottons, silks, rayon, linen, or a blend of these fibers.

Take a good look at your wardrobe before selecting the color. If you don't have other suits, consider purchasing a neutral color that will blend with several colors in your wardrobe. If you have selected a pattern with a lot of detail, the details won't be seen as easily on dark colors campared to light colors.

> ☛ *Tip: I usually buy a little more than the pattern guide lists to allow for shrinkage, length adjustments, matching plaids, stripes, or patterns, and changes in the layout of the pattern pieces. If you purchase enough fabric for a pair of slacks and an extra skirt, you'll find that your jacket will have a longer life. I purchase fabric for an extra skirt because of fashion changes in skirt lengths, and weight fluctuation. You can always make another skirt and wear your jacket unbuttoned, if you should have a weight gain.*

Lining

The lining fabrics that I prefer for my jackets are rayon (Bemberg's Ambiance), polyester (Hang Loose), and China silk. Hang Loose has more body than Ambiance, which makes it easier to handle while cutting and sewing. If you're trying to build body into the suit jacket, Hang Loose is the best one to use, unless you live in a hot climate. When selecting the lining color, be sure to test it by slipping it under your suiting fabric. Sometimes, the color of the lining will alter the color of the suiting fabric.

To add body to skirts and slacks, I line them with Hang Loose, which is static free and keeps them from clinging to the body. Hang Loose comes 48" wide, and is less expensive than rayon or China silk. I'll often purchase Ambiance for the jacket and Hang Loose for the skirt and slacks, even if the colors don't match exactly.

Interfacings

Most tailors use several types of interfacings in a suit jacket, and that's what we'll be doing in this book. For the front of the jacket, and the under collar, I use Armo Weft fusible interfacing. It works well with lightweight to heavyweight suiting fabrics. You'll need approximately 1 1/2 to 2 yards for a suit jacket. You'll also need a lighter weight interfacing for the front side panel, uppercollar, front facing, back neck facing, and hem allowances. I recommend either SofBrush, or Whisper Weft fusible interfacings. You'll need approximately 1 1/2 to 2 yards for a suit jacket. All these brands of interfacing are available in several colors, which makes it easier to match the fabric so it won't show through on the right side of the garment, or change the color of the suiting fabric. They also have the right amount of body and flexibility for a suit jacket, are dry cleanable, and stay fused to the suiting fabric, instead of separating after several dry cleanings.

Pocketing fabric

I use silesia, the same type of pocketing fabric used in a man's suit jacket, in my jackets. Silesia is a tightly woven, thin, strong fabric that will make the pocket last longer, even if you have a tendency to put keys and coins in your pockets. I prefer the 100% cotton version, instead of a rayon and cotton blend (make sure you ask about the fiber content). Silesia comes in several colors. You'll only need about 3/8 to 1/2 yard for a suit.

Notions
● *Buttons*

It is important to choose buttons for your jacket carefully, because they can change the style or look of the garment. Buttons have either a gloss, or matte finish, and this should be considered when making your selection, as well as the size for both the front of the jacket and on the sleeves.

● *Thread*
Matching thread to your suiting fabric sounds like a simple task, but there a couple of things to be aware of. If the store has florescent lighting, as most do, check the thread color near a window, or where there is natural lighting. Quite often, florescent lighting distorts color. Lay a strand of the thread on the fabric to test. If you cannot find an exact match, purchase thread a little lighter than a light-colored fabric and a little darker than a dark-colored fabric. You'll probably need 3 spools of thread for the suit.

● *Twill tape*
Twill tapes come in two colors, black and white, and in many different widths and fibers. The type needed in tailoring is 100% cotton twill tape (this is what tailors use). Don't buy the poly/cotton type, because it is too heavy and doesn't shape easily. You'll need approximately 1 yard of the 1/4" cotton twill tape, and 1 yard of the 1/2" or 5/8" cotton twill tape.

● *Bias tape and muslin scraps*
For reinforcing the shoulder area and the armscye, you'll need some lightweight fabric scraps. The lighter weight grades of muslin or something similar will work well. You can also unfold cotton bias tape and use it for the upper half of the armscye instead of using bias-cut muslin strips (as described in

detail later). Press open the folded edges and cut a strip of the tape about 1/2" wide and about 8" to 10" long.

● *Sleeve wigan*
Sleeve wigan is an interfacing used in the sleeve hem allowance of men's suits. It is precut in 3"-wide bias strips, and is also available by the yard. The strip version can also be used to ease in the fullness in the sleeve cap (described later). Wigan comes in three colors, white, black and gray. You'll need approximately 1/2 yard of the 3" wide wigan for easing in the sleeve cap, and 1 yard for the hems.

● *Shoulder pads*
Shoulder pads come in many shapes and thicknesses, and many sewers are not sure what style pad will give them the best results. I've had excellent results using 1/2"-thick covered raglan shoulder pads in my jackets for both set-in and raglan sleeve styles. This type of shoulder pad gives the entire shoulder and sleeve cap area a very nice shape. It's important to purchase covered shoulder pads so that the suiting fabric won't stick to the pad, as it will to many uncovered pads. Shoulder pads come in three colors, white, black and beige.

● *Sleeve heads*
Sleeve heads can be purchased, or you can make your own. I'll describe how later.

Pressing Tools
A *pressing cloth* can be purchased, or you can make one yourself from muslin. It is used to prevent shine from appearing on the

fabric, and it helps protect the fabric from scorching.

A *seam roll* is used to press open seam allowances, preventing the edges of the suiting fabric from imprinting on the right side of the garment.

A *ham* is used for pressing curved areas without flattening them, for example, darts and seam allowances in the shaped areas of the jacket.

A *clapper* is used to hold in the steam and heat while pressing seam allowances, darts, and so on, without scorching, as I'll describe below.

A *point presser* is used for pressing right to the tip of pointed areas, and its base can be used in place of the clapper.

A padded *Tailor Board* is the best tool I've found for pressing the sleeve cap area, and it can be useful for pressing many other shapes in a garment, as well.

Optional supplies

Lightweight, non woven *fusible interfacings* are used for reinforcing pattern pieces. This is discussed in detail on page 9.

Cotton or poly/cotton *batiste* is used as an interfacing in the upper back half of the jacket. I use it in heavy coats, but usually not in suit jackets.

Heavy *muslin* is used to make a quick fitting version of the body and sleeve of the jacket

before cutting it out from suiting and lining fabrics, and will be discussed in detail on pages 9 and 10. ❧

For Tailoring Supplies by mail order, contact:

Sew-Pro Workshop
2315 B Forest Drive, Suite 50
Annapolis, Maryland 21401
(800) 355-1137
Fax (410) 798-1951

Chapter 2

Sewing Preparation

Suiting fabric

No matter what you select, your suiting fabric needs to be preshrunk. The easiest and best method is to send the fabric to the dry cleaners. Have the dry cleaners put the fabric through the normal dry cleaning and pressing cycle. This not only takes all the shrinkage out, but it also gets out any finish or sizing that may be in the fabric that could prevent the fusible interfacing from staying fused to it. The dry cleaner I use charges $12.00 for 4 to 5 yards length of fabric, and $18.00 for 7 to 8 yards of fabric.

I feel you get the best results from having the dry cleaner shrink and press your fabric. But, an alternative preshrinking method is to dampen a clean beach towel or sheet (run the towel or sheet through the rinse cycle of your washing machine), then lay the towel or sheet out flat, and place the suiting fabric on top (Figure 2.1).

Figure 2.1

Roll the two together like a bed roll, trying not to wrinkle the fabric any more than necessary (Figure 2.2). Leave the fabric wrapped in the towel for about 8 hours to dampen throughly, then remove the suiting fabric and lay it on a flat surface to dry. Do not hang the damp suit fabric for drying, because the weight of the damp fabric will cause it to stretch. After drying, steam press the fabric.

Figure 2.2

Lining fabric

Preshrink all lining fabric The easiest way to preshrink rayon and polyester linings is to soak them in warm to hot water for 5 to 10 minutes. Hang the fabric to drip dry, or put it in the dryer, then press it. Dip a silk lining in cool to luke warm water for a few minutes, and let it drip dry, then press it.

☞ *Tips: Purchase a pressure-fitting shower rod and place it in the middle position of the tub so the water dripping from the fabric drips directly into the tub, not on the edge. The shower rod can be removed until you need it again.*

Fusible interfacing

Preshrinking fusible interfacings can be quite confusing to many sewers. I've found two good ways to preshrink the fusible interfacings:

● *The Dip Method*
Dip the interfacing in warm (not hot) water for a few minutes. Gently squeeze out the excess water, and hang over a shower rod with the glue side up, to drip dry. Be careful of the water temperature! I tried dipping a 5-yard piece into hot water for 10 minutes, and found that the water felt slimy, which meant the glue had melted, and was floating in the water. It also meant that the fusible interfacing was probably not going to stay pressed to the suiting fabric for any length of time, which made the 5 yards of interfacing unusable.

● *The Steam Method*
If you have a steam iron that produces a lot of steam, use the following method for preshrinking: Set the iron on a high setting with maximum steam. Lay the interfacing flat on the ironing surface with the glue side up. Hold the iron about an inch above the interfacing and steam; you'll actually be able to see the interfacing shrinking. Allow the interfacing to dry before you move it.

Pocketing fabric

Silesia pocketing fabric doesn't really need preshrinking, and suit manufacturers don't bother to preshrink it. However, since the fabric is 100% cotton, it's easy (and safest) to preshrink it. Soak the silesia in hot water for 10 to 20 minutes, hang to dry, or dry it in the clothes dryer, then press it.

Twill tapes

Preshrink the twill tape by soaking it in very hot water for about 15 minutes. Wet twill tape can be dried in the dryer or left to air dry.

Muslin scraps

Be sure to preshrunk the muslin before

cutting the bias strips, etc. The easiest way is to run it through the regular wash cycle.

Sleeve wigan

Do not preshrink the sleeve wigan. Preshrinking will soften it, and makes it more difficult to handle when easing in the fullness of the sleeve cap.

PREPARING THE PATTERN

Patterns you'll use more than once store best if they're stabilized by fusing them to inexpensive non-woven interfacing. Even if you'll use them only once, interfaced patterns are easier to handle than plain tissue. They don't distort or shift as easily, and you can mark through them without tearing the tissue.

Cut the pattern pieces apart from each other leaving as much extra tissue around each piece as possible, and press each piece to remove creases. Position the individual pieces right side up onto the fusible side of the lightweight, non-woven, interfacing, and press to fuse the two together (Figure 2.3).

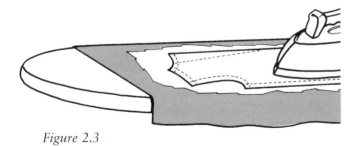

Figure 2.3

Press all the way to the cutting edge of the pattern pieces (this is why it's important to leave the extra tissue around the pattern pieces, so that the iron won't have to touch the glue

side of the fusible interfacing). After you have fused all of the pattern pieces, trim off the extra tissue that extends past the cutting edge of the pattern, unless you need to leave it on for alterations to your flat pattern.

Measure the pattern pieces for fitting purposes, and make whatever alterations are needed to the flat pattern. Also, check the hem allowances at the bottom of the jacket and the sleeves. If your pattern doesn't allow for a 2"-wide hem allowance in both places, add extra hem to bring it to that length. The extra weight this provides at the hem line will allow the jacket to hang better while being worn, and the hem of the sleeve will stay securely up inside the sleeve.

THE MUSLIN FITTING

I realize that you're anxious to get started on the jacket, and probably don't want to spend any time making a muslin version, but I'd like for you to try it just once. Making a muslin jacket for fitting purposes can be done quickly, and will save you much time in the long run. It also eliminates disappointment about the fit after the jacket has been finished. I think you'll find it a worthwhile investment of your time and effort.

The pieces needed for the muslin fitting are the jacket fronts, jacket backs, side panels (if your pattern has them), and the sleeves. You won't need anything else. Pin these pieces on the straight grain of the muslin and cut out. Using a fabric marker or pencil (I use a permanent marking pen), draw onto the muslin the center front line, the waistline mark, the roll line of the lapel, and the seam marks needed for sewing purposes (Figure 2.4). Sew

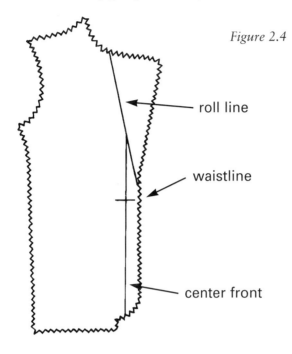

Figure 2.4

roll line

waistline

center front

all of the pieces of the body portion of the jacket together, press open the seam allowances, and clip seams where necessary.

Sew in one sleeve and try the jacket on. If you have trouble with the fit across the back, then you'll have to sew in both sleeves. Trim both layers of the seam allowance from 5/8" to 1/4" at the lower half of the armscye. Turn up the hem allowances at the bottom of the jacket and the bottom of the sleeves, and either pin them in place, or sew them by machine with large stitches (Figure 2.5). Pin in the shoulder pads you'll be using in your jacket, and the muslin jacket is ready to try on. The best way to do this is to try it on over top of a silky blouse so the muslin will slide, instead of sticking to the body, and will hang better for checking the fit.

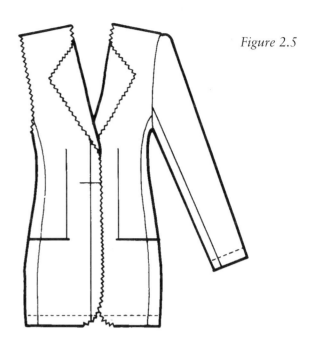

Figure 2.5

Line up the center front lines and waist line marks, pin the jacket closed, and fold back the lapel. Check your sleeve length, the length of the body of the jacket, the shaping and circumference at hip and bust areas, the fit across the back, and the slope of the shoulder line. Make note of any further adjustments to the flat pattern that are needed, and make them after the next step.

Determining lapel ease

Finally, examine the jacket at the fold line of the lapel. Usually, the fold line will bow out away from the body, and this gaping can be controlled. This also occurs at the edge of the neckline opening on jackets without a lapel, from the shoulder down to the top button.

Here's how to find out how much the lapel or edge needs to be taken in so that the jacket won't gape: Pinch out a tuck at the fold line or edge to pull the jacket close to the body and pin to hold the tuck in place (Figure 2.6), then measure the tucked area, and write its length down. This will be the

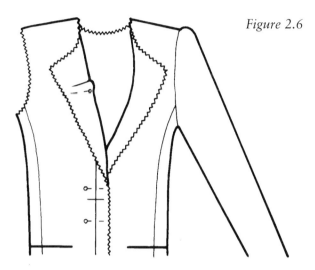

Figure 2.6

amount of fabric that needs to be eased in at this area to keep the jacket close to the body. I'll cover this in detail during the construction phase of the jacket. ❧

Chapter 3

Cutting Out the Pattern

Place the pattern pieces on the straight grain of the fabric and pin in place. I don't like to use the folded edge of the fabric, because that edge can become stretched or distorted (even if preshrunk) and this will show up on pieces, such as the center front of the skirt, that should be cut on the fold. If any of your pattern pieces are supposed to be cut this way, create a new fold just for them. Cut out each piece with a good pair of scissors, or a rotary cutter if you prefer.

Place the upper on straight grain of fabric and the under collar on the bias (even if the pattern calls for the straight grain of fabric).

Cutting stripes and plaids

If you have chosen a striped, plaid, herringbone, or other regularly patterned fabric for your jacket or suit, pay close attention to the lines of the stripe, plaid, or other pattern. As you lay out the pattern pieces, make note of the position of the fabric pattern at the center front, center back, collar ends and center back, sleeves, pockets, and the lapel area, and change them if they are unattractively positioned, or won't match adjacent pieces. I usually choose to position a plaid line at the hemline. The one area that I have frequently missed in the past has been the lapel edge, so I'll pay particular attention to it now.

The outside edge of the lapel should be placed as parallel to the striped, plaid, or herringbone weave as possible. In order to accomplish this, you probably won't be able to place the entire facing on the straight grain of fabric (Figure 3.1).

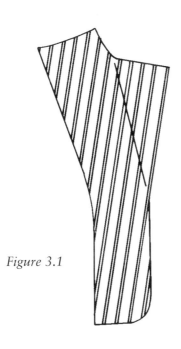

Figure 3.1

If you find that the grain line is way off below the lapel area, then split your facing pattern piece so that the lower half can be placed on straight grain of fabric, while the upper half can be positioned parallel to the straight lines of the stripe, plaid, or herringbone. The best place to split the facing pattern is

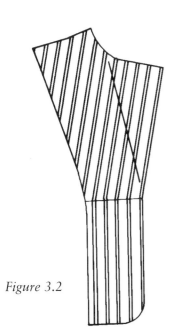

Figure 3.2

at the first (top) button, either in the middle of the button if you are making bound buttonholes, or just below it if you're making machine buttonholes (Figure 3.2).

When dealing with this situation, I always cut the interfacing on the straight grain even though the suiting fabric may be off grain. This will help stablize the facing piece that's off grain. Cut the interfacing in one piece, then split it where the pattern is split, so you don't have to fuse across a seam.

☛ *Tip: I had an opportunity to visit a men's wear factory where they made very fine suits with prices starting at $595.00 for ready to wear. One of the many things I noticed was the cutting area. The suits*

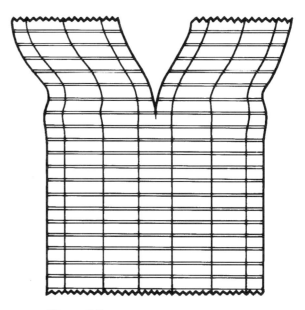

Figure 3.3

were cut by hand with several layers placed right sides together on top of each other, and some of the layers were stripes and plaids. They handled this by splitting the 60" wide fabric as near the fold as possible, making sure they were cutting in the center of a lengthwise plaid or stripe line (Figure 3.3). *Then they placed one layer of the same fabric onto the cutting table, and placed a few 2" x 2" boards, cut approximately 30" to 36" long, across the fabric in several places to hold it in place.*

The next layer was placed carefully on top of the first layer starting at a crosswise plaid line while lining up the lengthwise lines. After the first few inches were lined up exactly, a board was placed there to hold it in place, and the underneath board was removed. They moved down the yardage a few more inches lining up the plaid or stripe lines and placed another board (Figure 3.4).

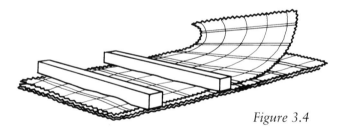

Figure 3.4

This was done throughout the 4 or more yards of suiting fabric. Even though you're only working with 2 layers of fabric, this is a very useful method. The sticks are handy for controlling slippery fabrics like linings, too.

After the pattern pieces have been cut, you can make your clip marks, chalk marks, etc., to mark notches, dots, darts, etc. on the jacket back and sleeves. Do not mark the jacket front, side panels, front facing, upper

collar, and under collar at this time. That will be done after the interfacing has been fused to the suiting fabric, so you don't lose any of your marks during the fusing. Also, the fabric can become a little distorted while pressing the fusible interfacing to it. Placing the chalk marks after fusing will give you better accuracy, especially at the pocket and buttonhole areas.

CUTTING THE INTERFACING AND LINING

Fusable interfacings are used on the front body of the jacket, and on collars, facings, and hem allowances. To match the different requirements of each area of the jacket, we'll use two different weights of interfacing; Armo Weft, a suit-weight interfacing; and SofBrush or Whisper Weft, which are lighter weight. I have the best results by using these brands and weights. Armo Weft will perform quite well even on a very lightweight suiting fabric. If it appears to be a little stiff after fused to the suiting fabric, don't be concerned, it will soften after you have your suit dry cleaned.

Cutting Armo Weft

The two pattern pieces that you'll cut from the Armo Weft will be the under collar and the jacket front. If the jacket front is one continuous piece extending to the side back, cut the entire piece from Armo Weft (Figure 3.5).

Fold under the hem allowance of the jacket front pattern, pin it to the Armo Weft on straight grain (Figure 3.6), pin the under collar to the Armo Weft on bias (Figure 3.7),

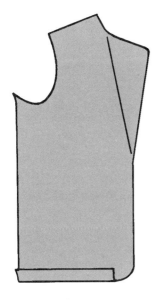

Figure 3.5

and cut. Trim off approximately 1/4" to 3/8" of the interfacing's seam allowances so there will be enough of the interfacing to be included in the stitching line of the seam allowances, but not so much that the glue from the fusible interfacing gets on the iron and ironing board cover. It won't harm the suit if you don't trim away the seam allowances of the interfacing because when the seams are pressed open correctly, over a ham or seam roll, neither the bulk nor the edges of the seam allowances will show on the right side of the garment.

Cutting Sofbrush or Whisper Weft

The pattern pieces to be cut from SofBrush or Whisper Weft are the front side panel (if your pattern has one), the upper collar, and the facing (Figure 3.8). You'll also need bias strips cut 1-7/8" wide, if you have allowed a 2" hem allowance as

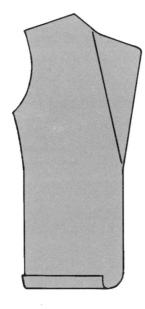

Figure 3.6

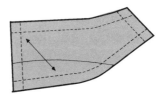

Figure 3.7

recommended. Measure the hem lengths of the sleeve, the sleeve vent area, and the hem allowances of the back and side back of the jacket and cut enough bias strips to fuse to each hem allowance. Trim off approximately 1/4" to 3/8" from the seam allowances of the side panel, upper collar, and facing interfacing.

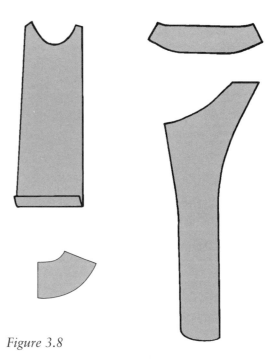

Figure 3.8

Cutting the lining fabric

Place the lining pattern pieces onto the lining fabric on the straight grain of the fabric, pin it in place, and cut out. I use pinking shears to cut out the lining, except for the neck edge and armscye, to keep it from raveling while working on the suit jacket. If your pattern doesn't have separate lining pieces, you'll have to use the jacket pattern pieces. Fold under the hem allowances of the jacket and sleeves. Then add 2" at the center back of the jacket (1" each side of the seam, if there is one) to create a 1" pleat. The pleat can either taper to nothing at the waist area, or run the full length of the jacket back.

FUSING THE INTERFACING

☛ *Tip: Here's how to protect your ironing surface and iron when fusing. Purchase 2 to 3 yards of muslin. Cut several pieces the length and width of your ironing board to place over the cover while fusing interfacings, and several pieces 18" x 24" to use as pressing cloths. Serge the edges, if you have a serger, or cut out the pieces with pinking shears. Wash and dry the muslin pieces before using to remove any odor and sizing in the fabric. These muslin pieces can be washed and dryed with your regular wash many times over to remove gummy residue from the fusible interfacing.*

Lay the jacket front, wrong side up on the ironing surface, and the interfacing, glue side down onto the wrong side of the suiting fabric. These pieces should be placed on the ironing surface as straight as possible.

Press the two together, starting in the center of the interfacing (Figure 3.9). I hold the iron down on the surface applying considerable pressure for 12 to 15 seconds and pressing the steam button 2 to 3 times. Pick up the

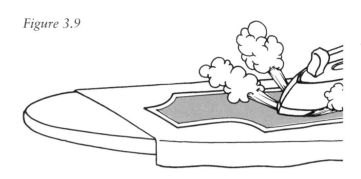

Figure 3.9

iron and work your way out to the edges of the fabric being fused (please note that you are pressing the interfacing not ironing it, so don't slide the iron side to side). Don't move the fused fabric until it has cooled completely (I cut out my lining pieces while I am fusing the interfacing to save time). A little steam is desired when pressing the interfacing to the suiting fabric, but don't let it get too wet.

Press the Armo Weft interfacing onto the jacket front and the under collar (Figure 3.10),

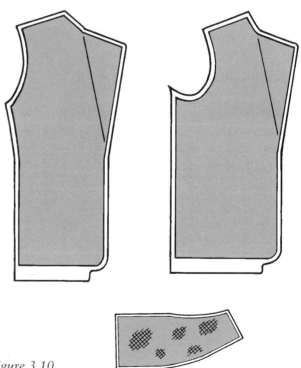

Figure 3.10

Figure 3.11

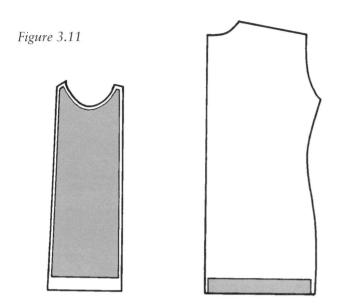

and the lightweight interfacing to the side panels (if any), the upper collar, the front facing (Figure 3.11), and to the hem allowances of the jacket back, side back panels (if any), sleeve vent and sleeve (Figure 3.12).

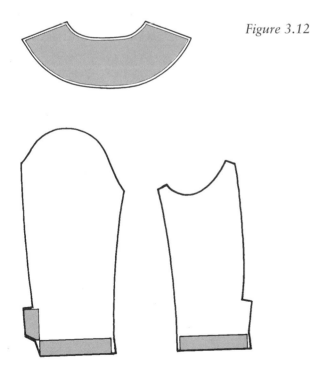

Figure 3.12

MARKING FABRIC

After the interfacing has been pressed to the suiting pieces, place the pattern pieces back onto them, and transfer all the necessary marks to them with tailors chalk. Mark the darts, the sleeve placement, the lapel roll line, pocket openings, buttons and buttonholes, and anything else needed for construction. If the jacket pieces seemed to be a little misshaped due to pressing on the interfacing, usually it's not enough to effect the jacket. Don't try to re-trim the pieces, or the jacket may shrink!

TEMPLATES FOR LAPEL AND COLLAR

This step can be eliminated if you're making a jacket without a collar or lapels.

Templates are patterns stiff enough to be used as stitching and marking guides for areas that need to be sewn or topstitched symmetrically and with perfect accuracy. They're commonly used by manufacturers and custom tailors to mark anything that has a precise and visible shape, such as the exact shape of the lapel area and the ends of the collar. These sections are on the bias of the fabric, and can stretch during the jacket construction, or while being worn, so they need additional interfacing. The templates I'll describe can also be used as patterns for these extra pieces. Manilla folders, oak tag, poster board, and quilter's template plastic are all good choices for template materials.

If you're using a manilla folder to make the templates, place the folder on a flat surface with the carbon paper on top, then place the pattern for the jacket front on top. Trace around the lapel fold line, and stitching lines (Figure 3.13). If you are using template

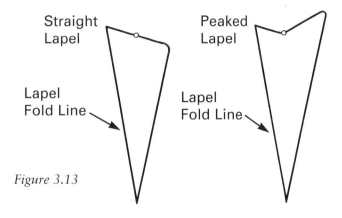

Figure 3.13

plastic, then place the template plastic over the pattern piece and trace the fold line and stitching lines for the lapel. Trace the ends of the under collar as shown.

● *Lapel template*

To indicate the grainline of the extra lapel interfacing pieces, draw a line on the template parallel to and about 1" away from the stitching line starting where the collar joins the lapel out to the point of the lapel (Figure 3.14). Before you cut out the template, label the point of the lapel and

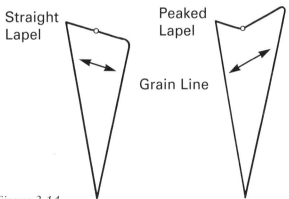

Figure 3.14

round it into the exact shape you want. Place a mark where the collar joins the lapel, label the roll line and put the pattern company's name and number on the template.

● *Collar template*

To create a template for the collar edge and point, position the under collar on the manilla folder or template plastic and trace the stitching line of the edge of the collar up to the point. To mark

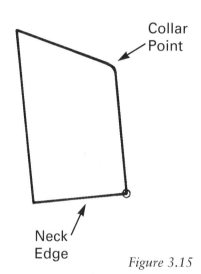

Figure 3.15

the shape of the extra interfacing, draw another line into the collar approximately 3/4" to 1" from the stitching line (Figure 3.15). Shape or trace the collar point, and draw an interfacing grain line from the neck edge, where the collar joins the lapel, to the collar point parallel to the stitching line

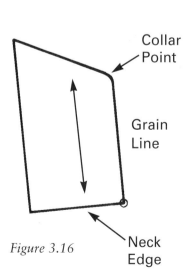

Figure 3.16

(Figure 3.16). Label the point and neck edge, otherwise you may not be able tell the neck edge from the collar edge. Place the pattern company's name and number on the template.

Reinforcing the collar and lapel

Using the templates as patterns, cut extra pieces of woven, fusible interfacing to reinforce the top of the lapel and the collar ends. Do not use a non-woven, weft, or knit. The interfacing must be the woven, fusible type only, such as Form Flex, and it's best if it's all-cotton.

Place the templates for the lapel and collar onto the interfacing on grain. Draw the shape of the top of the lapel and down the edge of the lapel approximately 1 1/2" to 2" with a pencil. Next, draw the shape of the

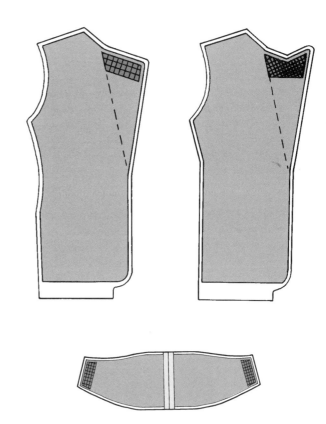

Figure 3.17

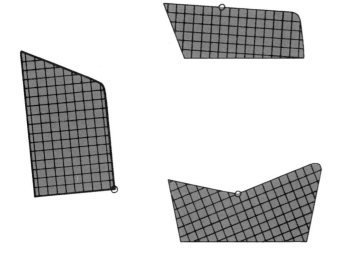

the 5/8" seam allowance, and trace around the outside of the template with a pencil. This pencil line becomes your guide line when stitching the front facing to the jacket front. ᛟ

collar template. This pencil line becomes your guide line when stitching the upper collar to the under collar. Cut out the interfacing (Figure 3.17), and fuse it to the top of the lapel at the collar edges seam allowance (Figure 3.18).

Lay the template for the lapel onto the wrong side of each jacket front allowing for

Chapter 4

Sewing the Jacket

THE JACKET FRONT

Wind 2 to 3 bobbins with the matching thread and thread your sewing machine. Set the stitch length on the sewing machine to a short stitch length, and stay-stitch the neck edge of the jacket front a scant 5/8" from the raw edge of the neck area, starting at the shoulder line and stitching towards the end of the lapel.

Set your stitch length on your sewing machine to a medium setting. Sew the jacket front to the side panel, if your pattern has a side panel. Clip the seam allowances at the curved areas (if your fabric frays easily, clip the seam allowance on an angle, rather than horizontal to the stitching line).

For the easiest construction of the pockets, the jacket front and pocket area should be kept as flat as possible until they're completed. If your jacket pattern has darts in the front, don't sew them now, unless the darts go beyond the actual pocket area. Many darts end right at the pocket and can be sewn after the pocket construction has been completed.

Pressing

Pay close attention to the following instructions, because we'll use variations on this method when pressing all the different parts of the jacket and suit throughout its entire construction.

Press all garment seams flat first, as sewn, before opening them, to meld the stitches into the fabric (Figure 4.1). Then position

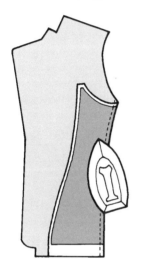

Figure 4.1

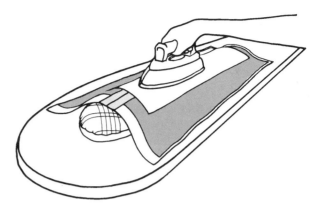

As soon as the iron is set down, replace it with the clapper, holding it on the seam allowances and applying a little pressure for a few seconds (Figure 4.3). Allow the seam allowances to cool, then move on to the next section.

the seam over a seam roll or ham. Open the seam allowances with your fingertips and place the pressing cloth over them (I usually reach for a purchased see-thru pressing cloth if I've got one). Press with a steam iron, then remove the pressing cloth and examine the opened seam to make sure it is pressed open fully and the seam allowances are smooth and flat (Figure 4.2).

Place the pressing cloth back on top of the same seam allowance, and this time have the clapper (or the base of the point presser) ready so that you can place it onto the seam allowance as soon as you've pressed and steamed the seam and can remove the iron.

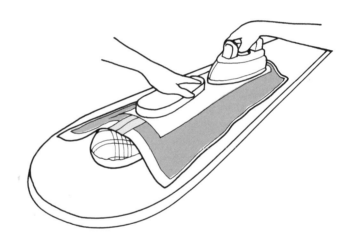

Reinforcing the shoulder

The shoulder area should be reinforced now to prevent the shoulder seam from stretching. Cut a strip of very lightweight cotton or poly/cotton fabric (a scrap of silesia or lightweight muslin will work) on the straight of grain approximately 12" to 15" long and 1/2" to 5/8" wide. Measure the shoulder seam line of the jacket front from the intersecting seam at the neck edge to the armscye seam and cut each strip slightly shorter than that to eliminate bulk where the seams intersect. Sew each fabric strip so it's centered over the seam line, stitching 1/2" from the raw edge of the shoulder seam using a regular stitch length (Figure 4.4).

Figure 4.4

Reinforcing the armscye

The armscye of the jacket needs to be reinforced more than any other area of the jacket because of the stress that it receives while being worn. The upper half of the armscye is reinforced with bias strips instead of twill tape to allow for some movement, and to make it easier to press open the seam allowances. The lower half of the armscye is reinforced with 1/4" cotton twill tape to prevent that area from stretching and changing its shape.

Starting with the upper half of the armscye, cut bias strips from the same fabric you used

for the shoulder seam (very lightweight cotton, silesia, poly/cotton, etc.) 1/2" to 5/8" wide and 10" to 12" long. Or, you can use double-fold cotton bias tape by pressing out the folds and cutting it to the size just specified for the bias fabric strips. Like the shoulder reinforcements, sew the bias strip to cover the armscye seam, stitching 1/2" from the raw edge and staying out of the seam intersections at the top of the armscye.

The lower half of the armscye is reinforced with 1/4" twill tape. The easiest way to do this is to press the 1/4" twill tape into a curved shape. Place the curved twill tape 1/2" from the raw edge and sew in the seam allowance so that the tape, but not the stitching, will be caught in the sleeve seam (Figure 4.5).

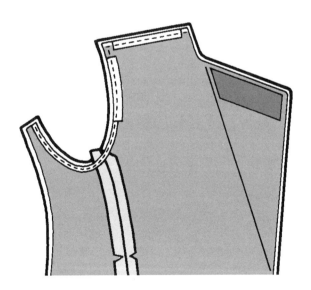

Figure 4.5

POCKET CONSTRUCTION

Pocket flap

Here are the key considerations when you want to make a professional looking pocket flap:

- First, the pocket flap must be the exact width as the opening of the pocket, so accurate cutting and sewing is a must.

- Second, the pocket flap can either be lined with the suiting fabric, or with lining fabric. Lining fabric is the better choice when you're working with a heavy suiting fabric, as it reduces bulk. If you use lining, the color of the lining should be the same as, or very close to, the color of the suiting fabric.

- Third, whatever you use underneath, the underside of the pocket flap should not be seen from the top. This can be achieved by adding 1/16" to the sides and bottom of the top pocket flap to make it larger than the original pattern (Figure 4.6), and by

Figure 4.6

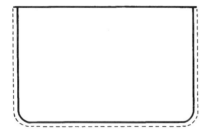

removing 1/16" from the sides and bottom of the lining pattern to make it smaller (Figure 4.7) (because we're changing both pieces in opposite directions, the total size of the finished flap does not change). I make two new pattern pieces from the original pattern,

Figure 4.7

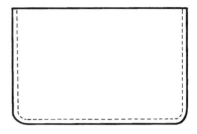

one for the top flap and one for the lining. Fold each flap in half and make a small clip top and bottom in the seam allowances at the fold so you can match the centers and distribute the difference evenly on both sides.

The top pocket flap should be interfaced. You can use either a lightweight, fusible interfacing (SofBrush or Whisper Weft), or a medium weight, sew-in, non woven interfacing. If you are using a fusible interfacing, press the interfacing to the wrong side of the top flap (Figure 4.8). If

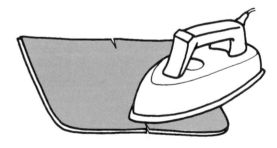

you are using the sew in interfacing, pin or baste the interfacing to the wrong side of the top flap. In either case, include the seam allowances in the interfacing.

☞ *Tip: You'll see many references, in the directions to come, to easing, and to which side of the construction should go next to the feed dogs when sewing. That's because there are many situations where one side of a seam is intentionally cut longer than the one it needs to be sewn to. This creates the shaping so essential to fine tailoring. The longer side needs to be "eased" onto the shorter side, so they both come out the same at the end of the seamline. The easiest way to accomplish this is to let the machine help.*

Since the feed dogs always tend to move the fabric on the bottom faster than the presser foot will allow the fabric on top to move, the bottom layer is always being slightly eased onto the top layer, but in an uncontrolled way. To control the amount of ease, always put the long side on the bottom, but as you sew, hold the layers in front and behind the needle, stretching them slightly so the short side is the same length as the longer one.

When sewing any long straight seams, eased area, and around curves, stop every 3" to 4" with the needle down and raise the presser foot. This relaxes the tension caused by the uneven action of the feed dogs and presser foot.

When sewing any long straight seams, eased area, and around curves, stop every 3" to 4" with the needle down and raise the presser foot. This relaxes the tension caused by the uneven action of the feed dogs and presser foot.

When sewing the top flap to the bottom flap, pin right sides together, lining up the clip marks and all seam allowances (Figure 4.9). Sew the pocket flaps together with the lining on top and the top flap next to the feed dog,

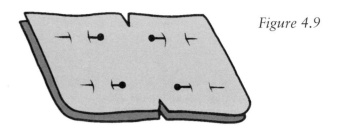

Figure 4.9

easing in the top flap while sewing (Figure 4.10). Grade trim close to the stitching line, press the seams flat, then open, then turn and press the finished flap.

Figure 4.10

To **grade trim** *means to trim the seam allowances after sewing so that the one next to the top layer is about 1/4", and each one below it is progressively narrower.*

Creating the double welt pocket

The normal width of a double or single welt pocket is between 5 1/2" to 6" for a women's suit jacket. It is important to keep the pocket size the original width given on the pattern. If you need to add extra width to the garment in the hip area, don't let the pocket width increase in size, or it will have a tendency to drop open while being worn, and may look a little strange.

There are two methods of double welt pocket construction explained in this book. Both methods produce professional looking pockets and are easy to handle, because all the stitching lines and welt widths are established before you cut, so you can confirm that everything is accurate before proceeding, and nothing can move or shift.

Method One, which uses only the pocketing as a stabilizer, is slightly easier to understand. Method Two, which uses wigan or Pellon as a stabilizer, looks slightly better because the welts crease more crisply. You should try them both out sooner or later, and I recommend making a sample pocket of either one before you proceed to the garment fabric. If you are using silesia for your pocketing fabric, you can use Method One or Method Two. If you are using some other pocketing fabric, I recommend using method two. In each case, the quantities given assume you're making two pockets.

■ Method One

Step 1. Measure the width of the pocket opening on the pattern. Cut four pieces of pocketing fabric (silesia) the width of the pocket opening plus 1 1/4" (for seam allowances) and about 8" long. For example, if the pocket opening is 6" wide, then the four pieces of silesia should measure 7 1/4" wide and 8" long (Figure 4.11). Adjust these lengths if your jacket pattern requires shallower pockets.

Step 2. Cut two strips of suiting fabric for the double welts the width of the pocket opening, plus 1 1/4", and 4" long (Figure 4.12). Cut bias strips if the fabric is patterned, or

straight-grain strips for plain fabrics (or if you prefer to match the pattern to the jacket body). Cut two pieces of interfacing

Figure 4.11

for the welt fabric strips the same size as the welt strips. You can use lightweight fusible interfacing such as SofBrush, or Whisper Weft, cut on straight grain (this is easier to

Figure 4.12

handle), or a non-woven, sew-in type of interfacing, such as medium-weight Pellon, which gives crisper results. If using a sew-in interfacing, pin or baste the interfacing to the wrong side of the fabric strips that form the welts, and handle the two as one.

Step 3. Cut two more strips of suiting fabric the width of the pocket opening, plus 1 1/4" and 3" long (Figure 4.13). These strips are used to face the inside portion of the pockets.

Figure 4.13

Step 4. Check the marks for the pocket opening on both the left and right sides of the jacket fronts. First, press up the hem allowance of the jacket front. Then measure the opening at each end of the pocket down to the finished hem length (these measurements should be the same, unless the pocket is suppose to be on an angle). Second, measure the front end of each pocket opening closest to the edge (they should be the same on the right and left sides) (Figure 4.14).

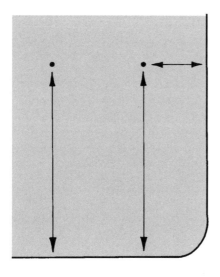

Step 5. Draw a straight, horizontal line on two pieces of the silesia, 1" down from the top, a little wider than the width of the pocket opening.
Draw two vertical lines approximately 1" long at each end of the pocket opening (this measurement should be the exact width of the pocket opening) (Figure 4.15).

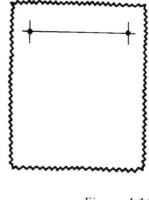

Figure 4.15

Step 6. Place one piece of the silesia onto the wrong side of the jacket front, lining up the chalk marks for the pocket opening, and pin in place, keeping the pins away from the pocket opening. Repeat for the other side of the jacket. Using a machine basting stitch (use the longest stitch on your machine and loosen the tension slightly), and sewing from the wrong side of the jacket, machine baste the pocketing fabric (silesia) to the jacket at the pocket opening directly on top of the line drawn in Step 5. Machine baste over the vertical lines to mark the beginning and end of the pocket opening (Figure 4.16).

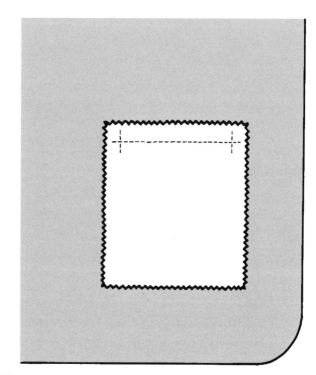

Figure 4.16

Step 7. Turn to the right side of the jacket, centering the fabric strip that forms the welts on the machine basted stitching lines. Pin in place (staying out of the stitching area) (Figure 4.17).

Figure 4.17   *Figure 4.18*

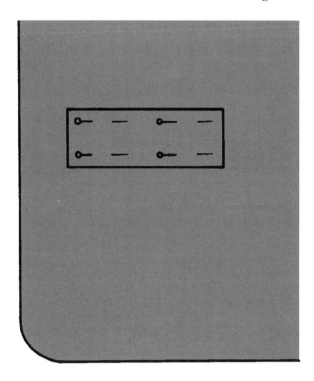

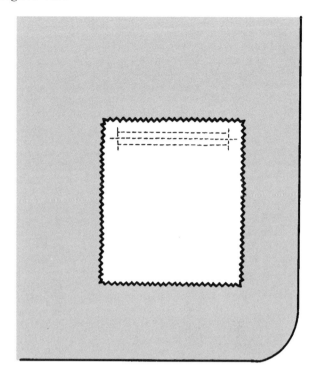

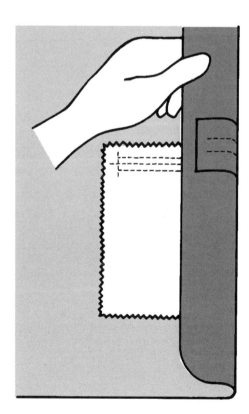

Step 8. Turn to the wrong side of the jacket. Sew two permanent rows of stitching (using a medium stitch length and normal tension), one row above the basted line (Figure 4.18), and one row below the basted line, starting and stopping at the vertical basted lines. The distance between the rows establishes the width of the pocket welts so they should be the same distance apart. The recommended width of the lip of the welt is 1/4", therefore, these stitching lines should be 1/4" apart. I use a presser foot that is 1/4" wide on one side as my guide, lining up the edge of the presser foot with the stitching lines. You can also draw these lines with a pencil directly onto the pocketing fabric (or interfacing, if using Method Two).

Machine baste two more rows of stitching, one row above and one row below the permanent rows of stitching, keeping all rows the same distance apart (Figure 4.19).

Figure 4.19

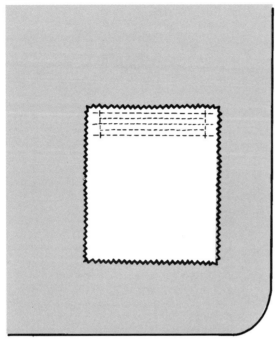

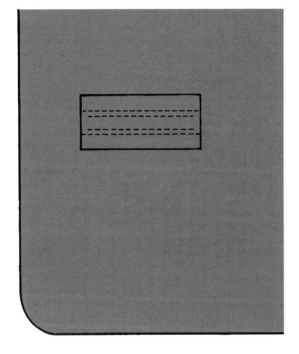

Step 9. Turn to the right side of the jacket front, and turn down the top portion of the fabric strip that forms the welt. Pin to hold in place (Figure 4.20). You can press the welt over, or simply pull it tight against the stitching at the fold. Turn to the wrong side of the jacket. Sew directly on top of the upper permanent

Figure 4.20

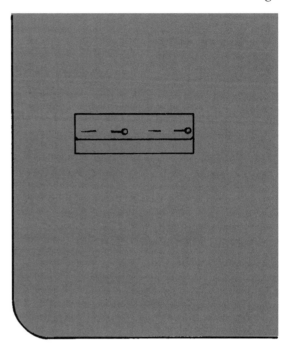

stitching line, starting and stopping at the verticle basting lines. This stitching line forms the upper welt (Figure 4.21).

Step 10. Turn to the right side of jacket front, and remove the pins from the upper welt fabric. Turn the lower welt fabric upwards, and pin to hold in place. Turn to the wrong side of the jacket. Sew directly on top of the lower permanent stitching line, starting and stopping at the verticle basting lines to form the lower welt (Figure 4.22). Remove the pins and examine the welt (Figure 4.23). Redo if necessary before cutting.

Step 11. Remove the upper and lower basting stitches. Lifting the loose welt edges

Figure 4.21

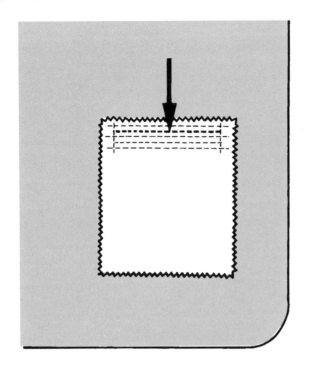

Figure 4.22

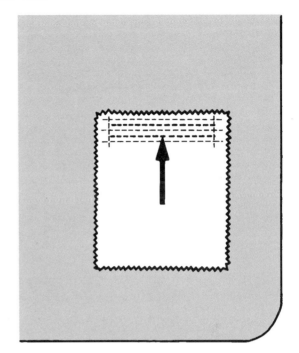

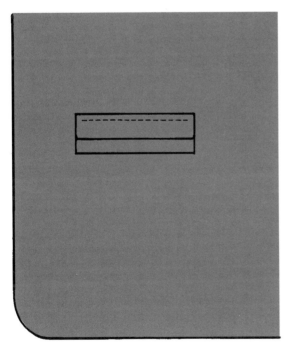

Figure 4.23

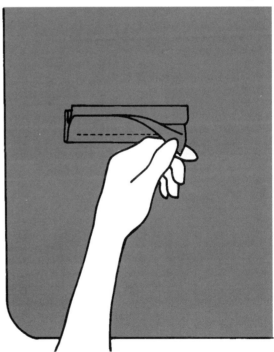

out of the way, cut open the pocket along the center basting line, clipping at an angle to form "V's" at each corner of the pocket (Figure 4.24). Note: You must clip the fabric

layers right to the stitching lines. Do not turn welts to the wrong side yet. Apply a seam sealant (such as Fray Check; test on a scrap first, checking that it doesn't spread or stain

Figure 4.24   *Figure 4.25*

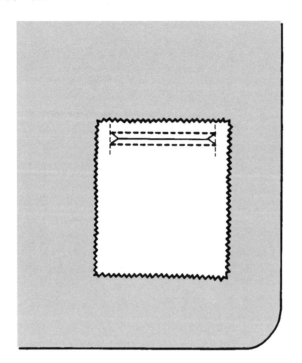

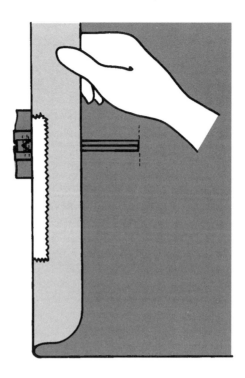

beyond where it's applied on your fabric!) to raw edges of "V's" to prevent raveling. Allow to dry before turning fabric to wrong side.

Step 12. Turn the fabric welts to the wrong side of the jacket and sew through the "V's" several times, starting at the cut pocket corners. Sew the next few rows away from the each other as shown (Figure 4.25). Press the welts. Serge the raw edge of the of the lower welt, or fold it under 1/4", and sew it to the pocketing fabric to form the inside facing (Figure 4.26).

Step 13. If your pattern doesn't have a pocket flap, then eliminate this step. Turn the jacket to the right side, and insert the seam allowance at the top of the finished pocket flap into the opening of the pocket. Place pins in pocket flap to hold (Figure 4.27). Turn to the wrong side of the jacket, and sew

the flap to the upper welt stitching line, directly on top of the previous stitching. Turn the fabric in such a way that you are

Figure 4.26

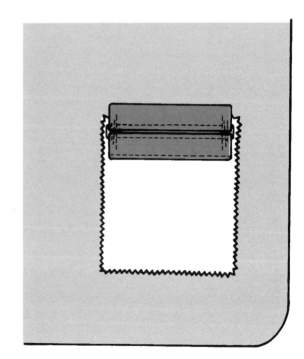

Figure 4.27   *Figure 4.28*

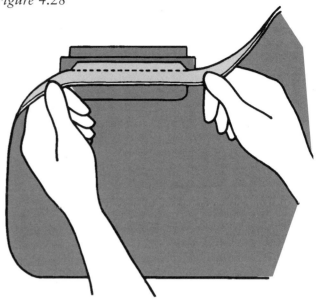

looking at the original line of stitching at the top welt when sewing (Figure 4.28).

Step 14. Baste the welts together (or to the flap) to keep them closed while constructing the rest of the pocket.

Step 15. Serge (or fold under) the lower edge of the facing strip, then sew it to the pocketing fabric that forms the inside of the pocket. Line up the pocket edges, and pin in place. Sew the inside pocket to the upper welt, sewing on top of the original stitching line (the same one you stitched over in Step 13) (Figure 4.29). Grade trim the seam allowances at the upper welt. Sew the sides of the pocketing fabric, and across the bottom.

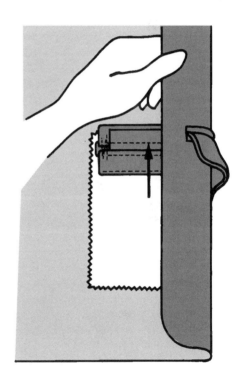

■ Method Two

Step 1. Cut two pieces of pocketing fabric the width of the pocket opening, plus 1 1/4", and approximately 5 3/4" long (these form

Figure 4.29

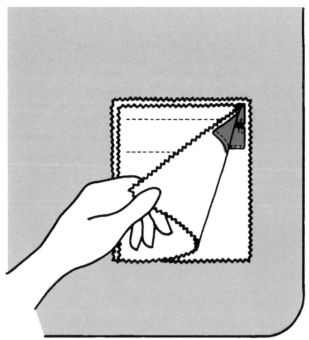

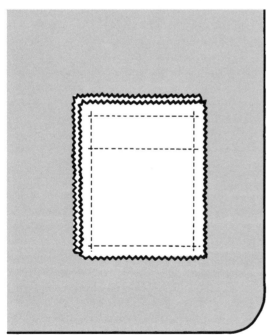

shallower pockets.

Step 2. In this method, the pocket opening should be interfaced with a sew-in type of interfacing only (do not use fusbiles).

(Pocketing Fabric)

Cut Two

Figure 4.30

You can use either wigan interfacing cut on straight of grain, or a medium-weight sew-in non-woven Pellon-type interfacing. Cut two pieces of the sew-in interfacing the width of

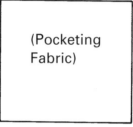

(Pocketing Fabric)

Cut Two

Figure 4.31

the pocket opening plus 2", and 3" long. For example, if the pocket opening is 6" wide, then cut the interfacing 8" wide and 3" long. Draw a line for the pocket opening in the center of the interfacing, extending the drawn line past the ends of the pocket opening. Draw two vertical lines to mark the ends of the pocket opening (Figure 4.32).

Figure 4.32

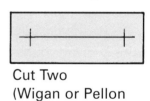

Cut Two
(Wigan or Pellon

Step 3. Cut two strips of suiting fabric for the double welts the width of the pocket opening, plus 1 1/4", and 4" long (Figure 4.33). Cut bias strips if the fabric is patterned (unless you prefer to match the pattern to the

Figure 4.33

Suiting Fabric

Cut Two

the outer pocketing layers) (Figure 4.30). Cut two more pieces of pocketing fabric the width of the pocket opening, plus 1 1/4", and approximately 8" long (for the inner pocketing layers) (Figure 4.31). Adjust these lengths if your jacket pattern requires

Suiting Fabric

Cut Two

Figure 4.34

jacket body), or straight-grain strips for plain fabrics. Cut two pieces of interfacing for the welt fabric strips the same size as the welt strips. You can use lightweight fusible interfacing (SofBrush, or Whisper Weft) cut on straight grain, or with a non woven, sew in type of interfacing (medium weight Pellon). If using a sew-in interfacing, pin or baste the interfacing to the wrong side of the fabric strips that form the welts, and handle the two as one. Cut two more strips of suiting fabric the width of the pocket opening, plus 1 1/4" and 3" long (Figure 4.34). These two strips are used to face the inside portion of the pockets.

Step 4. Check the marks for the pocket opening on both the left and right sides of the jacket fronts. First, press up the hem allowance of the jacket front. Then measure the opening at each end of the pocket down to the finished hem length (these measurements should be the same, unless the pocket is suppose to be on an angle). Second, measure the end of the pocket opening (horizontally) closest to the center front of the jacket to the edge (they should be the same on the right and left sides) (Figure 4.35).

Step 5. Position the interfacing on the wrong side of the jacket, lining up the chalk marks for the pocket opening. Pin in place. Machine baste interfacing to the jacket sewing at the pocket opening, sewing on the drawn line. Machine baste vertical lines to mark the

Figure 4.35

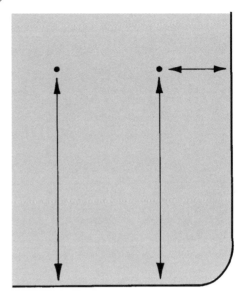

beginning and end of the pocket opening (Figure 4.36).

Figure 4.36

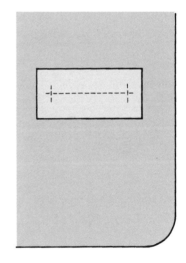

Step 6. Turn to the right side of the jacket, centering the fabric strip that forms the welts on the machine basted stitching lines. Pin in place (staying out of the stitching area) (Figure 4.37).

Step 7. Turn to the wrong side of the jacket. Sew two permanent rows of stitching (using

Figure 4.37   *Figure 4.38*

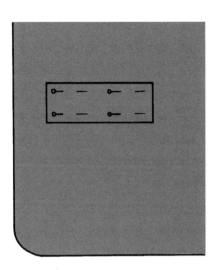

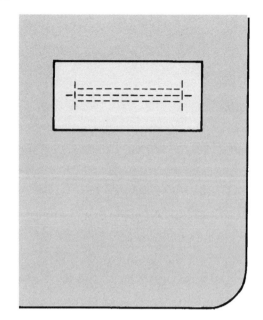

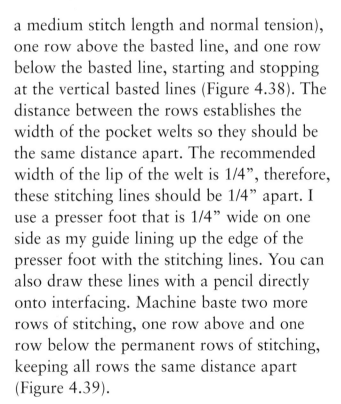

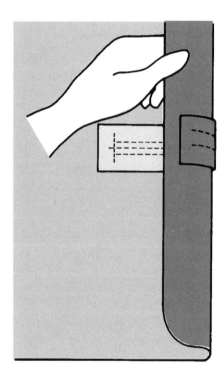

a medium stitch length and normal tension), one row above the basted line, and one row below the basted line, starting and stopping at the vertical basted lines (Figure 4.38). The distance between the rows establishes the width of the pocket welts so they should be the same distance apart. The recommended width of the lip of the welt is 1/4", therefore, these stitching lines should be 1/4" apart. I use a presser foot that is 1/4" wide on one side as my guide lining up the edge of the presser foot with the stitching lines. You can also draw these lines with a pencil directly onto interfacing. Machine baste two more rows of stitching, one row above and one row below the permanent rows of stitching, keeping all rows the same distance apart (Figure 4.39).

Step 8. Turn to the right side of the jacket front, and turn down the top portion of the fabric strip that forms the welt. Pin to hold in place (Figure 4.40). Turn to the wrong side of jacket. Sew directly on top of the upper permanent stitching line, starting and

stopping at the verticle basting lines (Figure 4.41). This stitching line forms the upper welt (Figure 4.42).

Figure 4.39

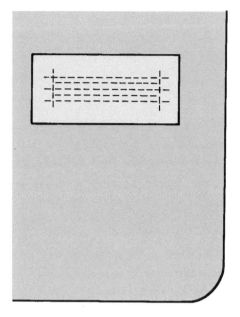

lower permanent stitching line, starting and stopping at the verticle basting lines to form the lower welt (Figure 4.43). Remove the pins.

Figure 4.40

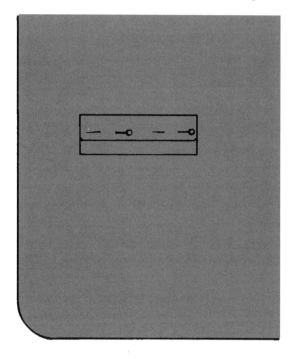

Figure 4.41

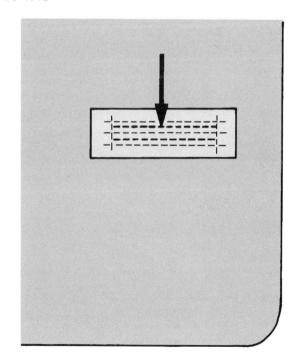

Step 9. Turn to the right side of jacket front, and remove the pins from the upper welt fabric. Turn the lower welt fabric upwards, and pin to hold in place. Turn to the wrong side of jacket. Sew directly on top of the

Figure 4.42

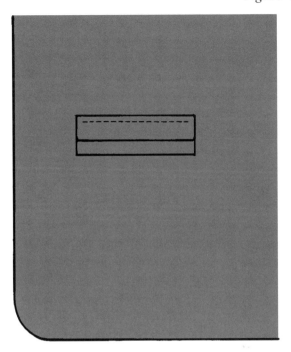

welts to wrong side yet. Apply a seam sealant (such as Fray Check; test on a scrap first, checking that it doesn't spread or stain beyond where it's applied on your fabric!) to raw edges of "V's" to prevent raveling. Allow to dry before turning fabric to wrong side.

Step 11. Turn the fabric welts to the wrong side of the jacket, and sew through the "V's" several times, starting at the cut pocket corners. Sew the next few rows away from each other as shown (Figure 4.45). Press welt. Serge or zigzag the raw edge of the lower welt, or fold it under 1/4", and sew it to the pocketing fabric to form the inside facing (Figure 4.46).

Step 12. If you've a flap, follow Step 13 in Method One. Sew pocketing fabric to inside facing of lower welt, under stitch, and press.

Step 13. Baste the welts together (or to the flap) to keep them closed while constructing

Figure 4.43

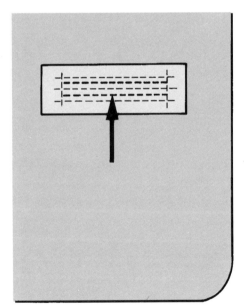

Figure 4.44

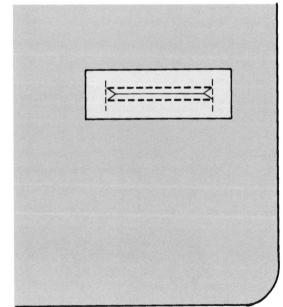

Step 10. Remove the upper and lower basting stitches. Lifting the loose welt edges out of the way, cut open the pocket along the center basting line, clipping at an angle to form "V's" at each corner of the pocket (Figure 4.44). Note: You must clip the fabric layers right to the stitching lines. Do not turn

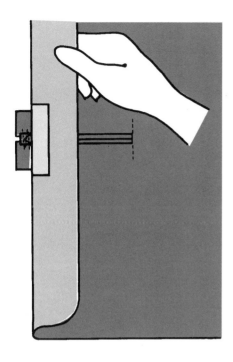

Figure 4.45

Figure 4.47

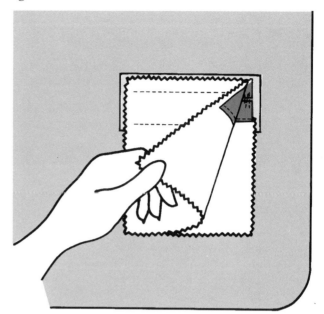

the rest of the pocket. (For clarity, the basting isn't shown in the illustration.)

Step 14. Serge (or fold under) the lower edge of the facing strip, then sew it to the pocketing fabric that forms the inside of the pocket. Line up the pocket edges, and pin in place. Sew the inside pocket to the upper welt (Figure 4.47), sewing on top of the original stitching line (the same one you stitched over in Step 8). Grade trim the seam allowances at the upper welt. Sew the sides

Figure 4.46

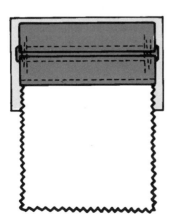

of the pocketing fabric, and across the bottom.

Single welt pockets

Use this method both for breast pockets and for regular pockets if you prefer the single welt look to the more traditional double welt pocket.

Because the single welt's ends are sewn to the top of the garment, the underside of the welt needs to be slightly smaller than the upperside, so add 1/16" to each side of the top half of the welt pattern, tapering to the original cutting line at the fold line. Then, subtract 1/16" on each side of the welt pattern on the underside of the welt tapering to the original cutting line at the fold line (Figure 4.48). Pin the

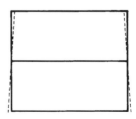

Figure 4.48

welt pattern to the suiting fabric and cut out.

Interface the top half of the welt with SofBrush, Whisper Weft, or sew-in Pellon-type interfacing (the underside half of the welt is not interfaced) (Figure 4.49). With

Figure 4.49

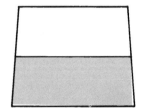

wrong sides together, sew the seam allowances of the welt together. Grade trim side seam allowances, press the seams open, and turn to the right side, pressing again.

Fold the welt in half again horizontally, towards the underside, and pin. While folded, machine baste across the raw edges at bottom of the welt (Figure 4.50). This

Figure 4.50

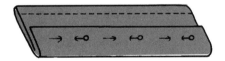

makes the upper side a little longer as well as wider, which helps shape it to the jacket; the basting holds the extra length in place.

Check the pocket placement marks for the single welt to make sure the pocket is aligned accurately (described in Step 4 of the double welt pocket construction). Pin the welt to the jacket front right sides together and with the raw edges up, matching the welt seamline to

the pocket opening. Machine stitch the welt in place, back tacking at the beginning and end of the welt (Figure 4.51).

Place the pocketing fabric (cut according to the pattern) onto the right side of jacket front, lining up the pocket opening marks with the lines

Figure 4.51

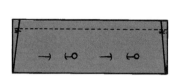

on the pocketing, and pin in place, staying clear of the pocket opening (Figure 4.52). Turn to the wrong side of the jacket, and sew on top of the first welt stitching line (Figure

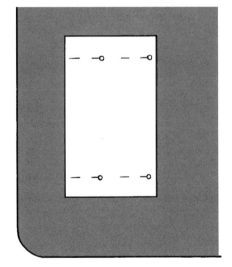

Figure 4.52

4.53). Turn to the right side of the jacket, and trim the welt seam allowance to 1/4". Sew another line of stitching approximately 3/8" above the first line (Figure 4.54). This stitching line should be 1/4" shorter on each end than the first stitching line.

Figure 4.53

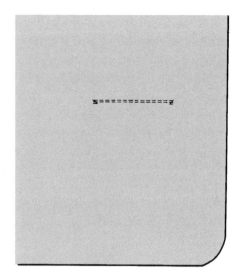

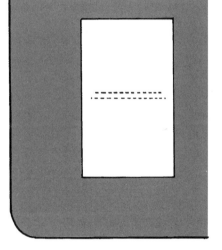

Figure 4.54

Cut open the pocket and through the jacket only, forming uneven "V's" at each corner (Figure 4.55). Apply seam sealant (such as

Figure 4.55

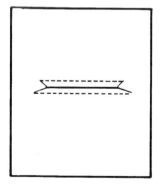

Fray Check; test on a scrap first!) to the raw edges of the "V's", and allow to dry before turning the pocket to the wrong side. Turn to the wrong side and fold down pocket fabric, then stitch down the "V's" starting at the clipped edge. Stitch several times with each stitching line further away from the previous stitching line (Figure 4.56).

Figure 4.56

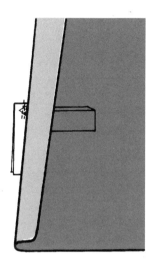

Sew the side seams and across the bottom of the pocketing fabric (Figure 4.57). Carefully press the pocketing fabric and welt. Machine-topstitch or hand-stitch the corners of the

Figure 4.57

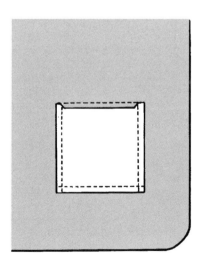

welts to the jacket front (Figure 4.58), then baste the welt closed to keep it from sagging while completing the rest of the suit jacket.

Figure 4.58

Patch pocket (with no stitching showing)

Cut out the patch pockets and lining from the pattern pieces. Fuse a strip of SofBrush or Whisper Weft to the facing portion of the pocket at the top (Figure 4.59). Sew the

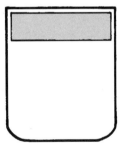

Figure 4.59

pocket lining to the top edge of the pocket facing, right sides together (Figure 4.60). Fold

Figure 4.60

the facing to the wrong side of the pocket, and fold the lining over the seam so the lining and pocket are wrong sides together (Figure 4.61). Stitch the two together around the

Figure 4.61

three unfinished edges 1/2" from the raw edge. This stitching line will become the guideline when you're stitching down the pocket.

☛ *Tip: You can make a template for stitching and pressing the patch pocket out of the paper template materials described in the Supplies list. Trace the shape onto the template material and carefully trim along the pocket stitching lines. Trace around the template onto the pocket to mark the final stitching line, then sew the guideline mentioned above exactly 1/8" outside it. Fold the pocket seam allowances around the template to use it as a pressing guide.*

Press under the 5/8" seam allowances using a pocket-curve template for accuracy. The stitching guideline should not show on the right side after pressing. Check the pocket placement markings (as described in Step 4 of the double welt pocket construction), then pin the patch pocket to the jacket front. Machine baste just the lower portion of the pocket, including the curves at each corner, using a long, wide zig-zag stitch and loosened

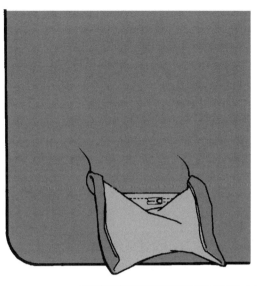

tension so that part of the stitch falls on the pocket and part on the jacket (Figure 4.62).

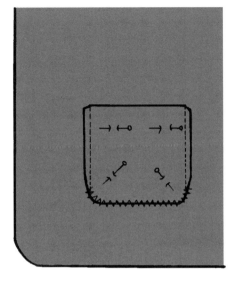

Figure 4.62

Figure 4.63

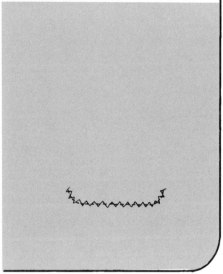

Next, remove the pins, lift and fold back the pocket, and using a regular straight stitch, machine stitch inside the pocket in the seam allowance between the guideline stitches and the fold, on top of the zig-zag stitches (Figure 4.63). Remove the zig-zag basting stitches and make another row of them to baste down the right side of the pocket (Figure 4.64). Lift the pocket again, and using a regular straight stitch, stitch inside the seam allowance on the right side, between the guideline stitching and the fold, and on top of the zig-zag stitches (Figure 4.65). Repeat the same procedure for the left side of pocket (Figure 4.66), and remove zig-zag basting after the pocket is completely stitched from the inside (remember to change the tension each time you switch from straight to zig-zag!).

Looking inside the pocket, trim the excess seam allowances to eliminate bulk. At the opening, tuck under the ends of the seam

allowances inside the pocket. Stitch down the corners by hand or machine to hide the raw edges and to reinforce the top of pocket (Figure 4.67).

THE BODY OF THE SUIT JACKET

Darts

Now that the pockets have been completed, you can sew the darts. Sew the darts within

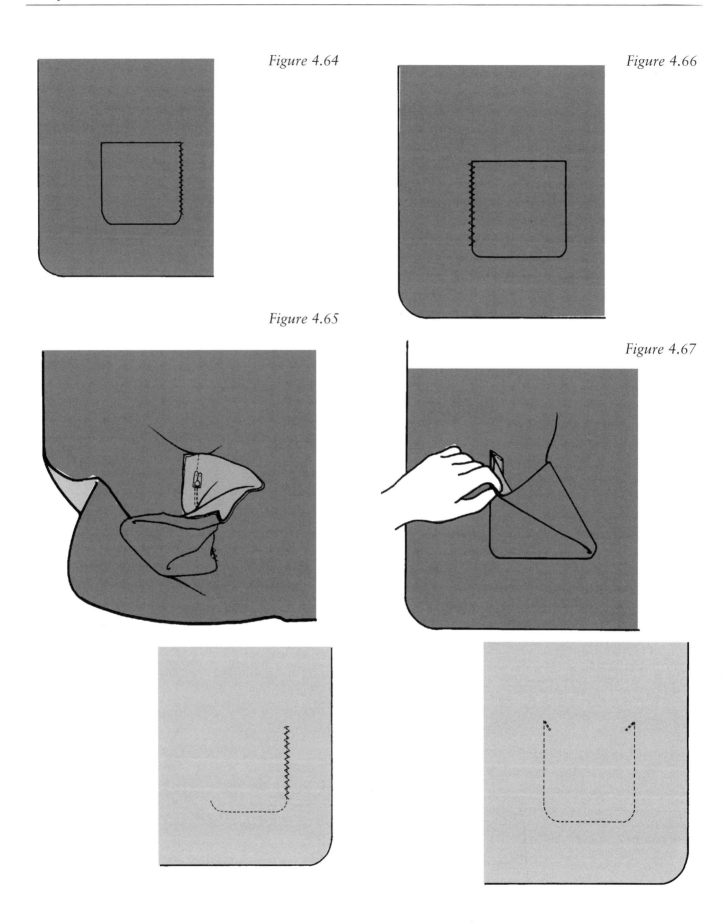

Figure 4.64

Figure 4.66

Figure 4.65

Figure 4.67

the body of the jacket in two stages. First, fold the dart in half and pin near the stitching line starting about the middle of the dart. Sew upwards to the very end of the dart, running off the end and continuing to sew for about an inch off the fabric to lock the threads. Return to the middle of the dart and sew towards the other end, running off that end for about an inch (Figure 4.68).

Figure 4.68

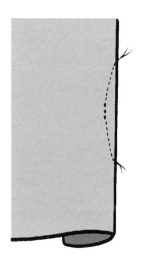

To press the darts as flat as possible, cut the dart at the fold line and out as close to the ends of the dart as you can without cutting into the stitching line. Press flat as sewn, then place the dart on a ham or seam roll and carefully open it with your fingers, then press open. Press the dart again using the clapper to hold in the steam and allow it to cool before moving it from the ham. If the dart is too narrow to cut open, or if the fabric ravels easily, then press the fold of the sewn dart towards the center front, and clip the fold at the widest part of the dart to enable it to press flat.

Bound buttonholes

Make the bound buttonholes before the back of the jacket has been sewn to the front. (Please note: the buttonholes for a women's jacket go on the jacket's right side.) Measure around the button you'll be using on the jacket to determine the size opening you'll need, then machine-baste stitching lines to indicate the width of the buttonhole, and the starting and stoping point for the buttonhole (Figure 4.69). Examine the basting lines to

Figure 4.69

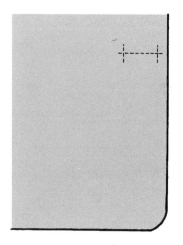

make sure the buttonhole is horizontal, and placed the correct distance from the edge of the jacket front (check this against the buttonhole placement lines on your pattern). If you have more than one buttonhole, make sure all buttonholes are the same distance apart, unless your pattern indicates otherwise.

Cut a square of the suiting fabric approximately 4" x 4" for each buttonhole (Figure 4.70), then fold the square diagonally in half, wrong sides together. Machine sew a straight line approximately 1/8" from the folded edge (this distance becomes the width of the lip for the bound buttonhole) (Figure

Figure 4.70

4.71). Cut off the excess fabric leaving a raw edge the exact distance from the stitching line as the stitching line is from the folded edge (Figure 4.72). You'll need two strips for each buttonhole, so cut the fabric strip in half and trim each half to equal the width of the buttonhole, plus 1".

Figure 4.71

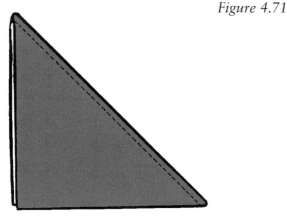

Figure 4.72

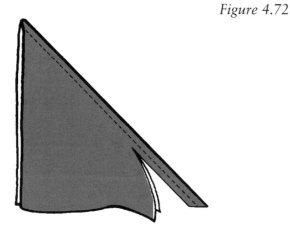

Working from the right side of the suiting fabric, place the raw edges of the fabric strips together exactly on top of the machine basting line (Figure 4.73) and pin in place.

Figure 4.73

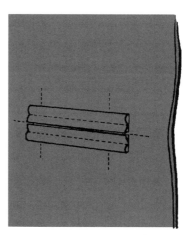

Make a pencil mark on the fabric strips indicating the starting and stopping points for the buttonhole (Figure 4.74). Then

Figure 4.74

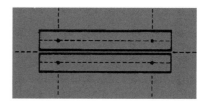

carefully sew right on top of the stitching lines on the fabric strips, starting and stoping at the pencil marks (Figure 4.75). Turn to the

Figure 4.75

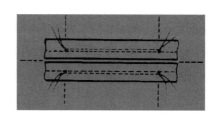

wrong side of jacket, and check the stitching lines against the basting lines for accuracy, correcting them if necessary.

Looking at the wrong side of the jacket front, cut open the buttonhole (don't cut the lips), forming "V's" at each end of the

Figure 4.76

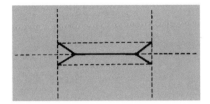

buttonhole (Figure 4.76). As always, you must cut all the way to the stitching line, or you won't be able to turn the buttonhole completely. Apply seam sealant to the raw edges of the "V's" and allow it to dry before turning fabric strips to the wrong side.

Turn the fabric strips to the wrong side and stitch across the V's about three times, stitching away from each previous stitching

Figure 4.77

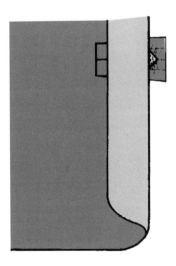

line (Figure 4.77). Press the buttonholes and hand-baste them closed if the buttonholes are large. You'll complete the back of the bound buttonholes after you've sewn the facing to the jacket front.

Controlling the lapel roll line

The area of the jacket front between the neck and the first button of a suit jacket is on the bias and has a tendency to stand away from the body. This happens to jackets whether they've got a lapel or not, and it can be easily controlled by easing out some of the fabric with twill tape. Since you made a muslin, as suggested on pages 9-11, you already know how much fabric to ease into the twill tape. (If you didn't make a muslin, on a single-breasted jacket you can allow approximately 1/2" of ease for an average bustline, and 3/4" to 1" of ease for a larger bustline. On a double breasted jacket, ease in approximately 1" for an average bustline, and 1 1/4" to 1 1/2" for a larger bustline. But you'll get the most accurate measurements from a muslin fitting.)

If you have not chalked the lapel roll line on the jacket front, place your pattern piece for the jacket front onto the wrong side of the jacket front and mark it now. Place a crossmark approximately 2" down from the top of the roll line near the neck edge, and another 2" above the break of the lapel at the bottom of the roll line. These mark the section of the roll line that you'll ease. To show how much you'll ease, place another mark on the roll line the same distance above the lower mark as your required ease (Figure 4.78).

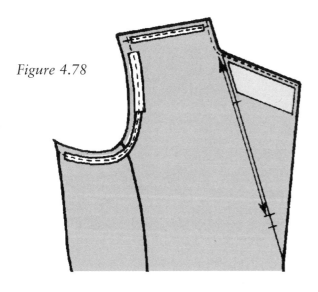

Figure 4.78

Starting at the top of the roll line and including the seam allowance, measure the roll line across the first mark and down to the ease mark, then cut two pieces of the 1/2" or 5/8" cotton twill tape exactly that length. Starting again at the top of roll line and including the seam allowance, lay the edge of the twill tape, without ease, against the roll line on the body side of the jacket (not the lapel side) down to the first mark. Pin in place to hold. Next, pin the lower end of the tape to the lowest mark (the mark 2" above the break of the lapel) (Figure 4.79).

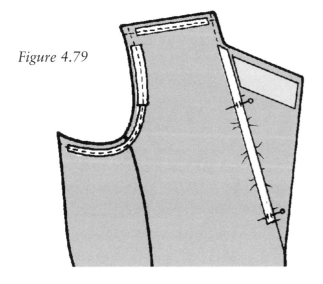

Figure 4.79

Distribute the extra fabric of the roll line (this is the amount you need to ease) between the marks at the top and bottom of the roll line, pinning in several places to hold the eased area to the tape. Hand stitch each side of the twill tape to the jacket with thread that matches the suiting fabric, picking up only a thread or two, so that stitches barely show on the right side (Figure 4.80). Press to blend in eased portion of the lapel.

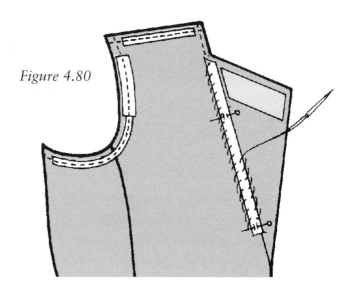

Figure 4.80

Controlling the jacket front without a lapel

Starting at the top of the jacket, place a mark at the jacket front seam allowance 4" down from the neck edge including the shoulder seam allowance, and another one on the seam line 2" inches above the first button. Make a third mark the same distance above the lower mark as the measured amount of ease you established in the previous section. Starting at the neck edge and including the shoulder seam allowance, measure the distance down to the mark indicating the amount of ease (Figure 4.81). Cut two pieces of the 1/2" or 5/8" cotton twill exactly that measurement.

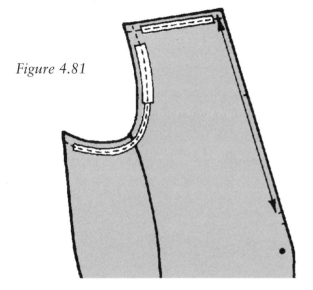

Figure 4.81

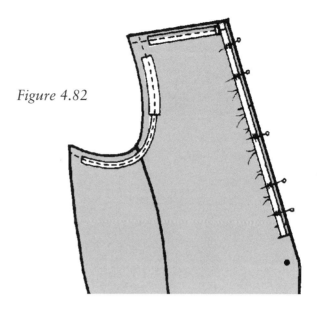

Figure 4.82

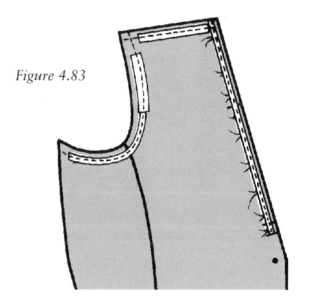

Figure 4.83

Starting at the top, and including the seam allowance, place the twill tape without ease down to the first mark so it's centered on the seam line and will be caught when the facing is applied. Pin in place to hold. Pin the lower end of the twill tape to the lowest mark (the mark 2" above the first button). Then, distribute the ease for the jacket front between the marks at the top and bottom of the seam allowance. Pin in several places to hold eased area (Figure 4.82). Machine stitch through the twill tape a scant 5/8" from the raw edge to hold the twill tape in place, and press to ease the fabric (Figure 4.83).

Sew the back sections of the jacket together at the center back. If the back of your jacket has separate side back panels, sew those to the jacket. Press open the seam allowances on a ham or seam roll, clipping the seam allowances

where necessary. Press the seam allowances again using a clapper to hold in the steam.

THE JACKET BACK

Sew a piece of 1/4" twill tape to the back neck area 1/2" from the raw edge, staying out of the shoulder seam intersection to eliminate bulk, but covering the neckline seam. As you did for the jacket front, sew 1/4" twill tape to the lower half of the armscye 1/2" from the raw edge, and sew a bias strip of fabric cut 1/2" wide to the upper half of the armscye, staying out of the seam intersection at the shoulder line (Figure 4.84).

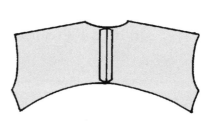

Figure 485

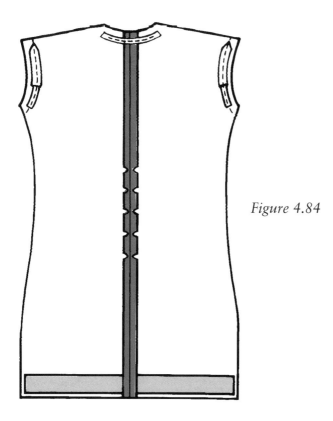

Figure 4.84

Pin the cotton batiste to the jacket back, and machine baste 1/2" from the raw edge at the neckline, shoulder seam, and armscye. Reinforce by sewing the twill tape to the neck edge and to the lower half of the armscye. It's not necessary to sew the 1/2" strip of bias fabric to upper half of the armscye (Figure 4.86).

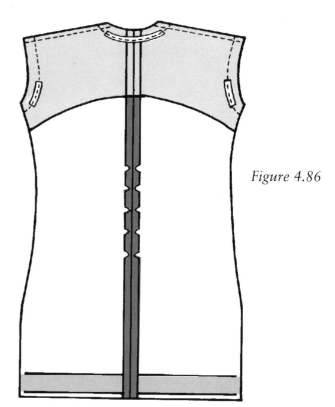

Figure 4.86

Interfacing the jacket back (optional)

If you're making a heavy jacket and choose to interface the back, do it before reinforcing the neckline and armscye. Make a pattern piece from the jacket back as shown, including seam allowances, then arrange the pattern piece on the cotton batiste on the bias so you don't restrict movement in the back of the jacket. Sew the center back seam, and press open the seam allowances (Figure 4.85).

Joining back to front

If you haven't cut the fusible interfacing strips and fused them to the back hem allowances, do it before joining the jacket back to the front. Cut bias strips from the SofBrush or Whisper Weft approximately 1 7/8" wide, if you've cut a 2" hem allowance. If not, cut the bias strips 1/8" less than the depth of the hem allowance.

Sew the jacket back to the jacket front at the shoulders starting at the neck edge and sewing down to the armscye. Because the back shoulder seam is longer than the front, sew with the jacket front on top and the jacket back next to the feed dog to ease in the shoulder area of the jacket back, stretching both seams slightly as you sew. The reinforcing tape will prevent overstretching. Press open the seam allowances.

Sew the side seams, or the side back seams, from the armscye down to the hem allowance. I stop with the needle down every 4" to 5" and raise the presser foot to relax the fabric layers, which helps to keep the top layer from ending up longer than the bottom layer. Press the seam allowances open, clipping where necessary to allow them to lay flat, then press again using a clapper.

THE UNDER AND UPPER COLLARS

Before sewing the under and upper collars to the jacket and jacket facing, you need to shape the under collar in relation to the upper collar to keep the under collar from pushing out and showing after the suit is finished. First, sew and press open the center back seam allowance of the under collar, then sew down the seam allowances on both sides next to the well of the seam to keep

them flat. Trim the seam allowances close to the stitching line (Figure 4.87).

Figure 4.87

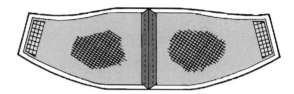

Shape the upper collar around the tailor's ham, with the right side of the collar next to the ham, pinning the neck edge of the upper collar to the ham starting at the center back clip mark. Push the pins straight into the ham to hold it in place (Figure 4.88). Then

Figure 4.88

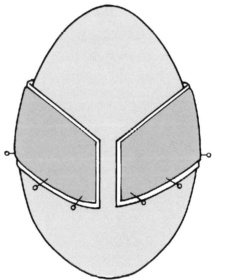

place the under collar neck edge on top of the upper collar, wrong sides together, and pin it into the ham starting at the center back seam allowance (Figure 4.89).

Check the ends of the under collar where the collar joins the lapel with the ends of the

Figure 4.89

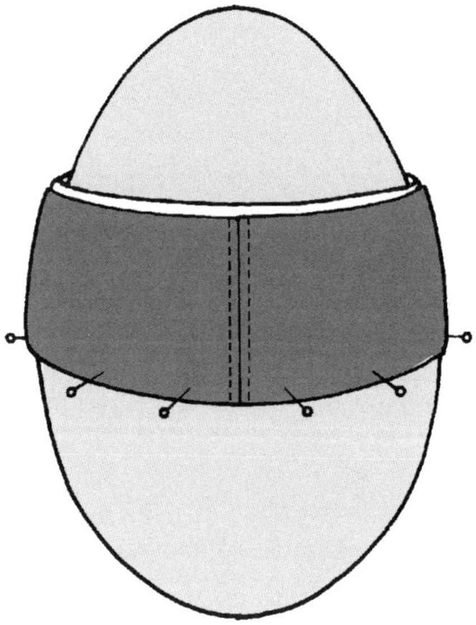

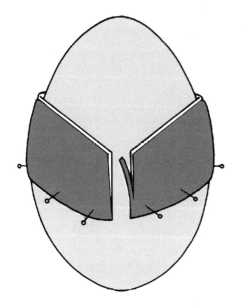

Fold back both the under collar and the upper collar at the collar roll line (Figure 4.91). The upper collar should be

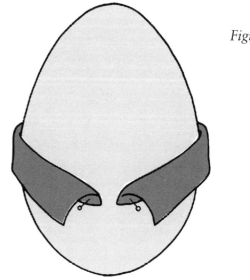

Figure 4.91

upper collar. The under collar should be approximately 1/8" shorter than the upper collar when sewing with a lightweight to medium weight suiting fabric. Cut off any excess under collar, if needed, to make the under collar smaller than the upper collar by that amount (Figure 4.90).

Figure 4.90

approximately 1/8" larger than the under collar along the entire outside edge of the collar. If the under collar is not smaller, trim off the excess under collar to make it smaller than the upper collar by that amount. If you're sewing with heavy fabric, the under collar should be smaller and shorter than the upper collar by 1/4" or more.

Under collar

With the collar pieces off the ham, place the collar template on the wrong side of the under collar 5/8" from the raw edge, and trace around the edge of the template to create a guideline for stitching the upper collar to the under collar several steps from now. I use an ordinary sharp pencil to get a thin, clean line that's easy to follow accurately and won't rub off.

Next, carefully pin the neck edge of the under collar to the neck edge of the jacket, matching notches, etc., and clipping the neck edge where necessary. Position them under the presser foot with the under collar next to the feed dog and the jacket on top, and starting at the end of the under collar at the center front, working towards the center back. Sew on the garment side of the stay stitching line and right next to it (this should be on the 5/8" seam line).

Repeat this same procedure on the other end of the under collar, sewing towards the center back (Figure 4.92). When I sew the

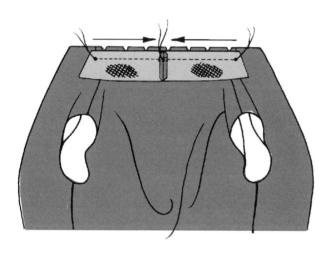

Figure 4.92

under collar to the neck edge, I stop every few inches with the needle position down into the suiting fabric to hold in place, then, raising the presser foot to adjust the under collar and neck edge to allow the fabric to relax. All of these techniques help ensure that each side of the collar will be eased equally. After the under collar has been sewn to the neck edge, carefully, press open the

seam allowances, clipping where necessary (Figure 4.93).

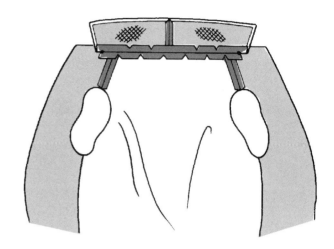

Figure 4.93

Upper collar

Sew the shoulder seams of the front facing to the back neck facing, right sides together, press open seam allowances, and trim them to 3/8". Pin the upper collar to the facing pieces, right sides together, matching notches and symbols, and clipping neck edge of facing where necessary. Sew the upper collar to the facing, with the facing on top and the collar next to the feed dog, starting at the ends of the collar and sewing to the center back of facing. Repeat the same procedure, starting at the other end of the collar and sewing to the center back. Press open the seam allowances, clipping where necessary (Figure 4.94).

The Four-point Closure

The Four-point Closure is a four-step technique for joining the collar and lapels that I learned in a "Bishop Method" sewing

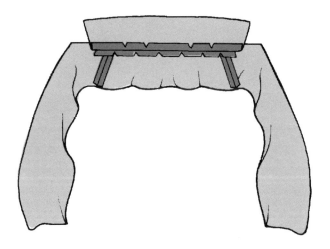

Figure 4.94

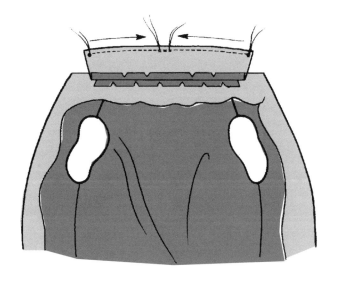

Figure 4.95

class I attended in the early 1960's. I still find that, when combined with using templates to ensure stitching accuracy, this is the best way to sew the collar and lapels together.

Step 1. Pin the upper collar to the under collar, right sides together, at the outside edge of the collar. Sew the two collars together with the under collar on top and the upper collar next to the feed dog, starting at the collar point, stitching directly on the penciled line traced from the collar template, and sewing to the center back of collar. Repeat the same proceedure, starting at the other end of the collar sewing to the center back of collar (Figure 4.95). Press open the seam allowances.

Step 2. Pin the front facing to the jacket front, right sides together, on each side of jacket, allowing for some ease in the facing at the break of the lapel (Figure 4.96) (fold the layers together on the roll line to see how much to allow, as described below).

In some cases, particularly with heavy fabrics, it's wise to check before going on that the facing is long enough at the hem after folding over at the roll line. Here's how to check: First, pin the wrong sides of the

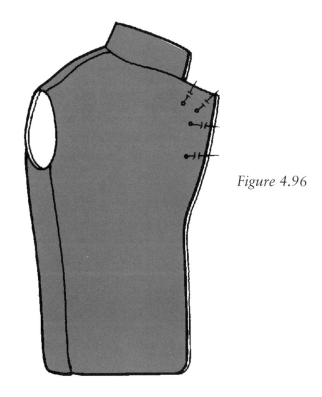

Figure 4.96

facing to the wrong side of the jacket front from the point of the lapel to just before the end of the break line, then fold over the lapel at the break line, allowing enough ease in the facing piece to fold over without pulling (Figure 4.97). If the facing is shorter at the

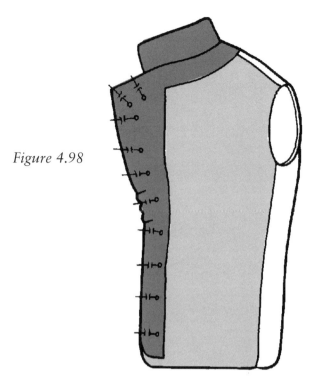

Figure 4.98

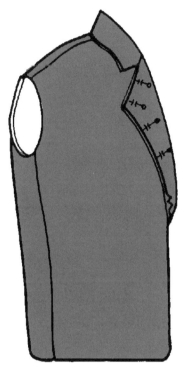

Figure 4.97

Carefully sew the upper part of the facing to the jacket with the facing next to the feed dog, and the jacket front on top. Starting at

bottom, adjust the facing seamline at the bottom of the jacket so the seam remains unchanged on the jacket front (for example, you may only have a 1/4" seam allowance left at the bottom of the facing when sewing the jacket seam at 5/8") (Figure 4.98). If the facing is too long, cut off the extra facing at the bottom (Figure 4.99). Next, place a chalk mark on the seam allowances of the facing and the jacket above and below the fold of the lapel. Remove pins, and re-pin the facing to the jacket front, right sides together, matching chalk marks above and below the fold of the lapel. Sew the facing to the jacket front following the instructions below.

Figure 4.99

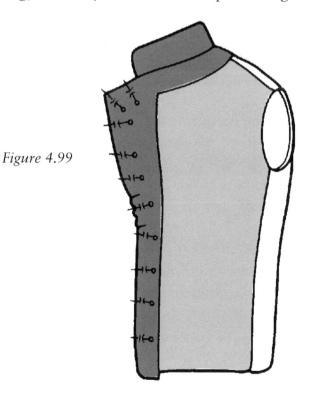

the point of the lapel and sewing on the penciled line you traced from the lapel template after fusing on the interfacing, sew down to the break of the lapel. I stop the machine every few inches with the needle down and lift the presser foot to adjust the fabric and to allow the fabrics to relax. Then complete the facing/jacket seam (Figure 4.100).

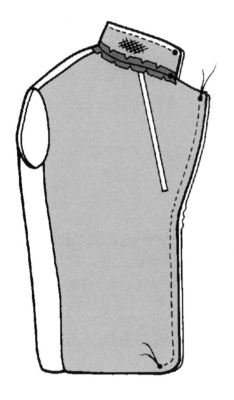

Figure 4.100

Press open the seam allowances of the facing and jacket front, using a pressing cloth and clapper. Grade trim the jacket/ facing seam allowances from the break of the lapel down to the hem, leaving the jacket seam allowance longer than the facing seam allowance. Don't trim the seam allowances of the upper half of the jacket until after the collar points are sewn together.

Step 3. Pin the facing to the jacket at the lapel area. Sew the two together, starting

exactly where the collar joins the lapel and sewing out to the end of the lapel point. Sew with the facing next to the feed dog and the jacket on top, sewing on the penciled line traced from the lapel template (Figure 4.101).

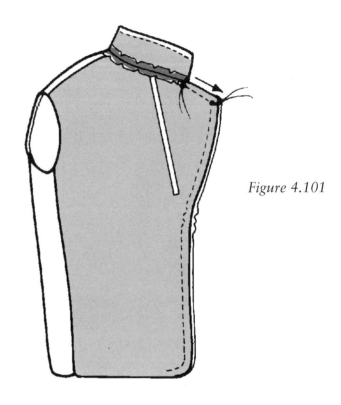

Figure 4.101

Step 4. Pin the upper collar to the under collar at the ends of the collar, matching all the raw edges. Sew with the upper collar next to the feed dog, and the under collar on top. Sew on the traced penciled line from the collar template, starting where the collar joins the neck edge, stitching to the point of the collar (Figure 4.102).

Press open the collar and lapel seam allowances, and grade trim. If there is a hole where the collar joins the lapel, hand-sew it closed. Turn and press again.

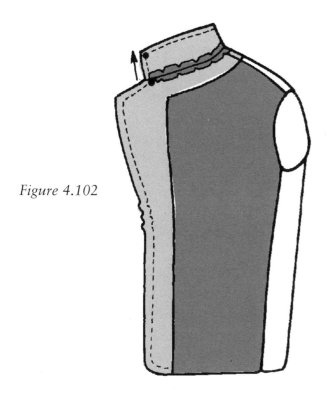

Figure 4.102

Pin the seam allowances of the neck edge of the jacket and facing together, starting at the ends of the collar and working towards the center back seam allowance. Sew the seam allowance together by hand or by machine using a long stitch length with the tension loose, starting at the ends of the collar sewing to the center back seam (Figure 4.103).

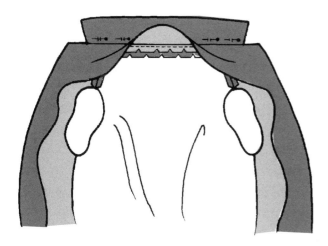

Figure 4.103

Jacket without a lapel and collar

Sew the shoulder seam allowances of the back neck facing to the front facing, press open and trim seam allowance. Pin the back neck facing to the back neck edge of jacket. Starting at the shoulder line, sew towards the center back, with the facing next to the feed dog and the jacket on top, sewing next to the stay stitching line. Repeat the same proceedure for the other side of the back neck facing (Figure 4.104). Pin the front

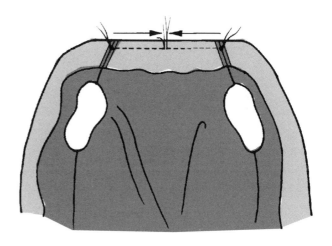

Figure 4.104

facing to the jacket front. If the facing is either too long, or too short, then make the adjustment within the hem allowance of the facing. Never force the facing to fit the jacket because the facing will cause the jacket front to pull towards the wrong side, if the facing is too short, and if the facing is too long, the facing will hang down and show on the right side of the jacket. Sew the front facing to the jacket front, right sides together, starting at the shoulder seam allowance, sewing with the jacket on top and the facing next to the feed dog (Figure 4.105).

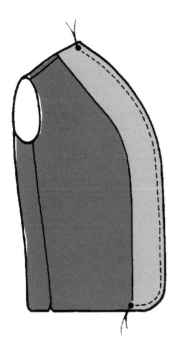

Figure 4.105

☞ *Very Important Tip: Stop every few inches wih the needle down as you sew the facing, and raise the presser foot to allow the two layers of fabric to relax.*

Press open the seam allowances, clipping where necessary at the back neck edge, and grade trim. Under stitch the facing making sure you are sewing through both seam allowances, starting at the shoulder line and sewing towards the center back. Under stitch the front facing, starting at the shoulder seam allowance and sewing down the front of the jacket facing. Press the facing and jacket front and allow to cool before moving.

BUTTONHOLES AND HEMS

The back of the bound buttonhole
Pin the facing to the jacket front at the buttonhole areas. Mark the opening of the buttonhole on the wrong side and right side

of the facing by pushing straight pins through each end of the buttonhole (Figure 4.106).

Figure 4.106

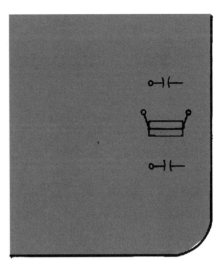

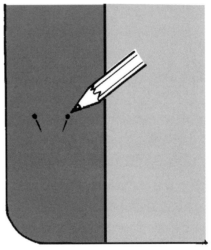

The traditional method
Cut a piece of organza 2" wider and longer than the buttonhole. Place the organza fabric strip on the right side of the facing, centering it over the markings for the buttonhole. Pin organza around the edges to hold in place. Push pins through the chalk marks for the buttonhole from the wrong side of the facing, and make chalk marks on the organza. Sew the organza to the facing using a small stitch length in a curved shape as

shown, sewing from chalk mark to chalk mark (Figure 4.107). Cut hole into the

Figure 4.107

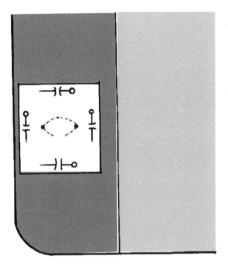

organza and facing close to the stitching line (Figure 4.108). Remove pins, turn organza

Figure 4.108

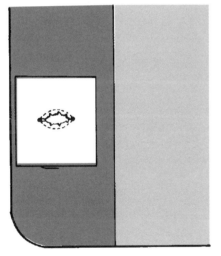

fabric strip to the wrong side and press. Pin the facing to the jacket front at the buttonhole area, and carefully hand stitch the opening in the facing to the buttonhole on the jacket (Figure 4.109).

Figure 4.109

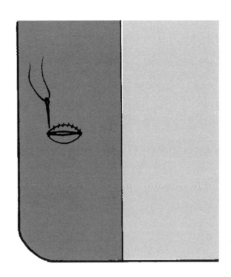

The fusible method

Cut a strip of SofBrush or Whisper Weft 2" wider and longer than the buttonhole. Place the fusible interfacing fabric strips on the right side of the facing with the glue side up, and pin in place. Make the chalk marks on the fusible fabric strips for the opening of the buttonhole, and sew the fusible fabric strips to the facing using a small stitch length.

Cut around the stitching line of the interfacing strip and facing, cutting close to the stitching line. Turn the interfacing strip to the wrong side of the facing, and carefully press in place so that no interfacing shows from the right side, and the fusible strip gets fused to the wrong side of the facing. Hand-stitch the opening of the buttonhole on the facing to the buttonhole on the jacket.

Machine buttonholes

If you are putting machine buttonholes on your jacket instead of bound buttonholes, you can sew them now, or you can wait until the jacket is completed. Check that the markings for the buttonholes are horizontal on the jacket front. You can use the traditional buttonhole style or the keyed buttonhole style. The keyed buttonhole style usually makes the jacket look more casual. Pin the facing to the jacket front near the buttonhole area to hold facing in place. Set your machine for buttonhole making, and sew the buttonhole. If once around by machine doesn't fully cover the buttonhole, then stitch around it a second time. Carefully cut open the buttonhole and clean out any excess fabric.

■ *Optional: For a more finished look, consider hand-sewing around the machine buttonhole with silk buttonhole twist, after the buttonhole has been cut open. Start at one end of the machine buttonhole, and hand sew on top of the machine stitching using the buttonhole stitch. Be sure to start with a long enough thread to completely cover the buttonhole. I usually cut my thread 24" long, and pull it through the bees wax to keep the thread strands together.*

Hemming the bottom of the jacket

This is the best time to sew in the hem of the jacket, after the facing has been sewn to the jacket, and before the sleeves are sewn in. If you haven't already pressed up the hem allowance, then I recommend doing this now. Pin the hem in place to hold it, and hand sew the hem allowance using a single strand of matching thread. You can use a catch stitch (Figure 4.110), which is recommended for fabrics that ravel easily, or a hemming stitch

Figure 4.110

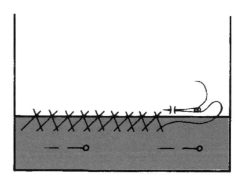

(Figure 4.111). Sew with the tension loose, and only pick a thread or two of the suiting fabric. When I had less sewing experience, I had a tendency to pull my thread too tightly, which made the stitching visible on the right side of the jacket. After the hem has been sewn, press it lightly from the wrong side.

Figure 4.111

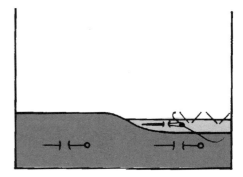

SLEEVE CONSTRUCTION

Two piece sleeve with a mitred vent

If you haven't made a muslin and checked the sleeve length, then you may not want to sew in the mitred vent until after you've tried on the jacket, with the sleeves sewn in and the shoulder pads pinned in place, to check the sleeve length. If you've already checked the sleeve length, then you can proceed with the mitred vent.

The upper sleeve

Press up the hem allowance of the upper sleeve only, and press over the vent. Mark the point of the sleeve vent with a chalk mark on the wrong side of the vent and the hem allowance. Clip through all layers of the hem allowances at the the raw edge where the hem allowance and sleeve vent cross, pointing the tip of the scissors toward the point of the sleeve vent (Figure 4.112).

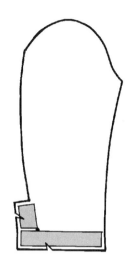

Figure 4.113

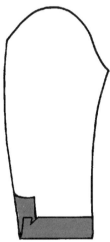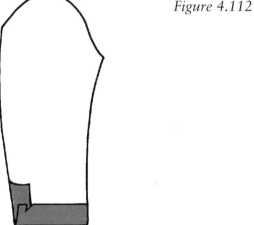

Figure 4.112

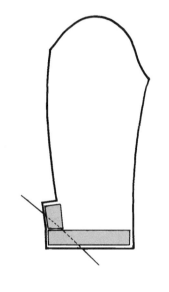

Figure 4.114

Unfold the vent and hem allowance (Figure 4.113), and draw a line on the wrong side of the fabric, from the clip marks to the mark for the point of the vent (Figure 4.114). This line becomes the stitching line which forms the mitered vent.

Pin the hem allowance of the vent to the bottom of the sleeve, right sides together, and sew on the line from the clip to the point (Figure 4.115), and sewing off the fabric for

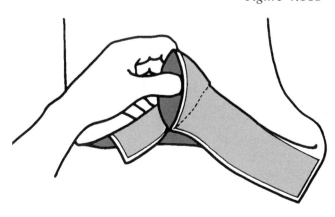

Figure 4.115

about an inch (the same way the ends of darts are sewn). Trim away the excess fabric leaving about 1/2" seam allowance (Figure 4.116), and cutting away a "V" shape at the

Figure 4.116

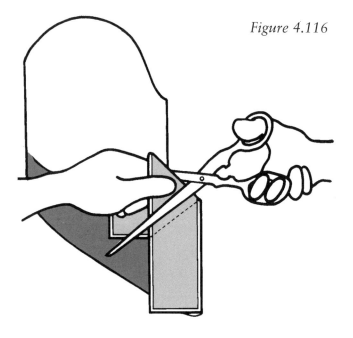

point of the vent to eliminate bulk. Press open the seam allowance on a point presser, if you have one (Figure 4.117), turn, then press again from the right side of the sleeve.

Figure 4.117

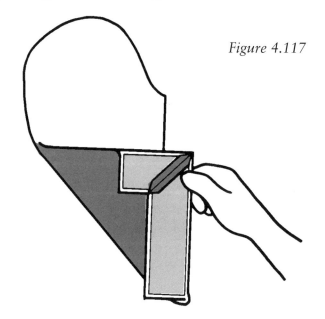

The under sleeve

Cut a square of interfacing approximately 1/2" x 1/2" from the woven, cotton, fusible interfacing. Press this onto the wrong side of the under sleeve at the opening of the vent to reinforce the seam allowance. This area will be clipped to the stitching line after the upper sleeve has been sewn to the under sleeve.

Sew the upper sleeve to the under sleeve, right sides together at the vent seam from the armscye edge down to the opening of the vent. Sew with the under sleeve on top and the upper sleeve next to the feed dog, easing in the elbow area. Back stitch a few stitches at the beginning of the vent to lock the seam, and press open using a ham or seam roll.

Fold up the hem allowance of the under sleeve making any adjustments necessary so that the hem allowance of the under sleeve lines up exactly with the hem allowance of the upper sleeve. Place a chalk mark or clip mark at the fold to use as your guide when sewing the seam allowance of the vent on the under sleeve (Figure 4.118).

Figure 4.118

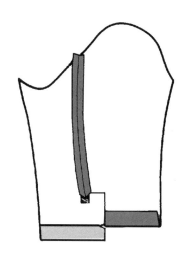

Turn to the wrong side of the under sleeve and fold up the hem allowance, and sew the vent seam (Figure 4.119). Press open the

Figure 4.119

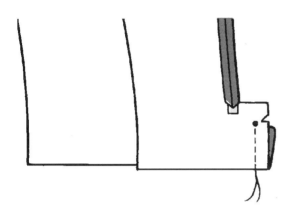

seam allowance of the vent, grade trim, then turn to the right side, and press again. (Figure 4.120) Do not sew the remaining seam of the sleeve. This will be done later.

Figure 4.120

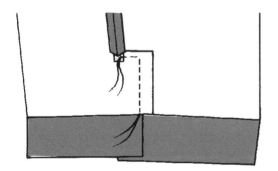

Sleeve vent buttons

While the sleeve is still flat is the best time to sew on the sleeve vent buttons. It's important to know where to place the vent buttons so that the jacket won't look homemade. I recommend that you make a template using the upper sleeve pattern piece.

Trace the shape of the finished upper sleeve in the vent area (do not include hem allowances). The template will be about 5" long and about one half the width of the upper sleeve at the finished hem area. If you are using 1/2" buttons at the vent, place a penciled dot 1 1/2" up from the finished hemline, and 5/8" from the finished vent edge. The next 2 or 3 dots for buttons will then be placed at 5/8" intervals above the first dot, and 5/8" from the finished vent edge (Figure 4.121). This will leave about

Figure 4.121

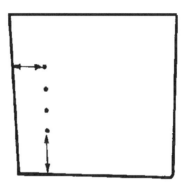

1/8" between each button, and 3/8" from the outside edge of the button to the finished vent edge, which is the correct spacing.

Make a hole in the template with an awl or similiar tool for the placement of each button. Lay the template on the finished sleeve vent on the right side of the fabric, and place a faint pencil mark inside each hole to mark the button placement. Center each button on a mark, and sew on the jacket (Figure 4.122).

If you're using buttons larger than 1/2" in size, place the button on the sleeve vent, leaving approximately 1 1/4" from the bottom of the button to the finished hem of the sleeve, and 3/8" from the edge of the button to the finished

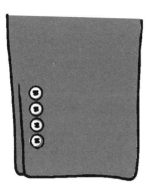

Figure 4.122

vent. Space the buttons so their edges are approximately 1/8" to 1/4" up from each other.

Easing in the sleeve cap

The best time to ease in the sleeve cap is while the sleeve is still flat, and before the last seam allowance of the sleeve has been sewn. The method I use is a little different from the traditional method, in which you put in two rows of basting stitches, and pull the thread to gather in the sleeve cap. Instead, I use strips of sleeve wigan (or necktie interfacing for heavier fabrics) cut on the bias.

If you have a half-yard or more of the 3" wide bias sleeve wigan, cut a piece approximately 15" (Figure 4.123) long. Fold the bias wigan

Figure 4.123

several times lengthwise, then divide the wigan in thirds lengthwise with two lines. Cut the wigan on these lines, through all the

Figure 4.124

layers (Figure 4.124). This will give you 3 pieces of bias wigan 15" long and 1" wide.

Starting on the wrong side of the sleeve fabric at the front of the cap where the notch or clip mark is located that indicates one end of the area to be eased, line up the edge of the wigan strip with the raw edge of the sleeve cap. Start sewing the 1"-wide strip of wigan to the sleeve cap 1/2" from the raw edge (inside the seam allowance), sewing with a medium stitch length. Sew 2 or 3 stitches to anchor the wigan to the sleeve cap, then stop with the needle down to hold the layers in place. Raise the presser foot, and stretch 2 or 3 inches of the wigan. Lay the stretched wigan down on the sleeve cap, and continue to sew the stretched wigan to the sleeve cap (Figure 4.125).

Figure 4.125

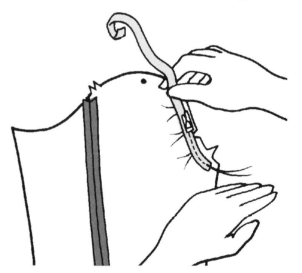

Repeat this process until you're 1/2" from the top of the sleeve cap. At the top of the cap, the wigan won't be stretched for a total of 1" (1/2" on each side). Lay the wigan flat in this area as you sew, then start stretching the wigan again, and continue to sew and stretch the wigan down to the notches or clip mark indicating the end of the eased area of the sleeve cap (Figure 4.126).

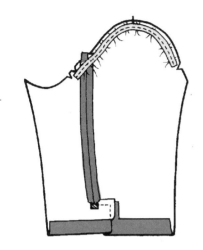

Figure 4.126

As soon as you pick up the sleeve cap, the stretched wigan will relax back to its normal shape prior to being stretched, which causes the sleeve cap to pull in. If you want to press the sleeve cap to press in the ease, place the sleeve over a "Tailors Board", being careful not to let the sleeve cap get stretched while pressing, or you'll be pulling out the eased portion of the sleeve cap. I don't press my sleeve caps until the sleeve has been sewn in the jacket.

If you are sewing with heavy fabrics, or Ultra Suede, substitute 1" wide bias strips of necktie interfacing for the sleeve wigan. Tie interfacing can be a little too heavy for regular suiting fabrics.

If you prefer not to use the sleeve-wigan method for easing in the sleeve cap, then sew two rows of basting stitches. The first row should be 1/2" from the raw edge of the sleeve cap, and the second 3/4" from the raw edge. Tie the rows together at one end to

anchor them, then, pull them from the other end to ease in the sleeve cap. Press the sleeve cap on a "Tailor's Board" to press in the ease.

Finishing the sleeve

Fold the vented sleeve lengthwise, and check to make sure that the seam allowance of the hem area doesn't stick out past the seam allowance of the sleeve. If it does, trim off the excess seam allowance in the hem area.

Sew the last seam allowance of the two piece sleeve, and press open. Sew the hem allowance of the folded-up hem to the seam allowance of the sleeve by machine on each side of the seam (Figure 4.127). This will

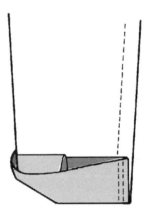

Figure 4.127

keep the hem allowance from falling down. Don't sew the hem of the sleeve to the sleeve; this will make the jacket look homemade.

Making a one-piece sleeve

Press up the hem allowance. Ease in the sleeve cap, using the sleeve wigan method, or the traditional two rows of basting stitches, and sew sleeve seam allowance following the instructions above for the last seam allowance in the two piece sleeve.

Sew the sleeve into the armscye

Pin the sleeve into the armscye, lining up the notches, etc. Check the eased portion of the sleeve cap to make sure the sleeve cap hasn't been eased too much. If it has, release some of the tension by carefully cutting through the wigan strip and stitching line with a small pair of scissors. Repeat this proceedure if more tension has to be released. If the sleeve cap requires more easing, pin it in as you pin the sleeve to the armscye.

Starting at the lower half of the armscye, sew in the sleeve 5/8" from the raw edge, using a medium stitch length, sewing with the sleeve next to the feed dog and the jacket on top. Stop the machine every few inches with the needle down, lift the presser foot, and adjust the layers. Continue to sew around the armscye, then check sleeve cap area for pinched gathers, and remove the stitching if necessary to remove them, then re-stitch (Figure 4.128).

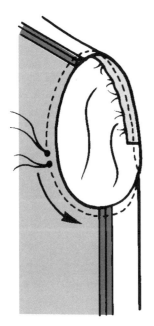

Figure 4.128

Sew a second row of stitches just inside the first in the lower half of the armscye only, to protect these seams against ripping. This area of the jacket receives more stress than any other. Trim the seam allowance at the lower half of the armscye to 1/4" in the area you stitched twice (Figure 4.129).

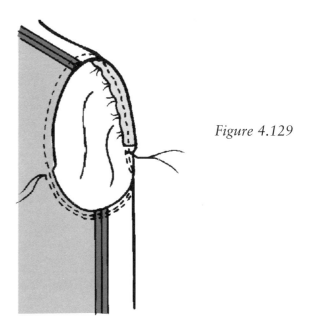

Figure 4.129

When you press sleeve cap area, you can either press open the seam allowance in the upper half of the jacket (Figure 4.130), or press the seam allowances toward the sleeve cap. The seam allowance is always pressed opened in a man's suit jacket, which gives a less-defined transition from shoulder to sleeve than is typical of women's jackets. If you prefer this look, feel free to press your seam allowances this way.

Sleeve heads

Sleeve heads add shape to the sleeve cap, and are placed into the sleeve cap from front notch to back notches, sewing the sleeve head to the seam allowance of the sleeve.

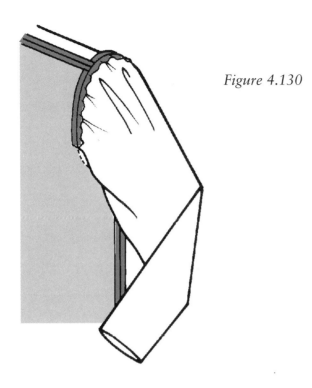

Figure 4.130

the bias fabric strip. Sew the two together 1/2" from the folded edge with a very long, loose stitch (Figure 4.131). The sleeve head

Figure 4.131

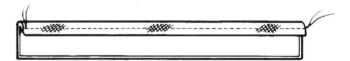

can be sewn in by hand, or by machine using a long, loose basting stitch, so that the sleeve head doesn't get compressed.

Line up the edge of the sleeve head with the raw edge of the seam allowance, and sew in the sleeve head close to the well of the seam. If you're sewing in the sleeve head by machine, you'll probably have to use your zipper foot. Sew with the sleeve head next to the feed dog, and the seam allowance of the sleeve cap only on top. Don't include the seam allowance of the jacket when sewing in the sleeve heads (Figure 4.132).

You can make or buy sleeve heads. I've had good results making my own for set in sleeves, using medium-weight polyester quilt batting in combination with covered, raglan, shoulder pads. Cut each batting sleeve head 2 1/2" wide and 16" long.

Purchased sleeve heads are made from several types of materials. The batting is either polyester, or cotton batting covered with a lightweight, loosley woven fabric such as muslin or cheese cloth, cut on the bias.

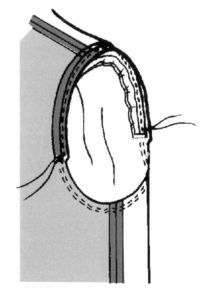

Figure 4.132

When making your own sleeve heads, the batting strip is cut approximately 2 1/2" to 2 3/4" wide and about 16" long, and the loosley woven bias strip of fabric is cut 3" wide and 16" long. The bias strip of fabric and batting are placed together and folded over at the top. This is done by folding over about 3/4" of the batting, and about 1" of

Sometimes firmly woven fabrics (and/or high-cut armscyes) cause wrinkles in the eased portion of the cap. You can eliminate the wrinkling by reinforcing bias-covered sleeve heads with bias strips of canvas. This is a common procedure used in a man's suit jacket. Please note: This method doesn't work well with uncovered polyester batting strips.

Cut 2 strips of canvas on the bias approximately 2 3/4" wide and 5" long, and label the strips "front". Cut two more strips of canvas on the bias approximately 1 3/4" wide and 5" long, and label the strips "back" (Figure 4.133). Place the "front"

Figure 4.134

Figure 4.133

strips on one end of the sleeve heads, and fold over 3/4" of the canvas. Sew in place 1/2" from fold line on sleeve head to hold. Place the "back" strips on the other end of the sleeve heads (but don't fold over the canvas this time), and sew 1/2" from fold line on sleeve head to hold in place (Figure 4.134).

When placing the canvas strips on top of the covered sleeve heads, keep in mind that you'll need a right and left sleeve head. Pin

the reinforced sleeve heads into the sleeve cap with the canvas placed next to the suiting fabric of the sleeve. Sew in place as described above.

Shoulder pads

Shoulder pads come in many shapes and thicknesses. Over the years, I have tried many different kinds with varying results. The two types I'll describe here are the ones I feel work best. The first is the 1/2"-thick, covered, raglan shoulder pad, and the second is the traditional shoulder pad that I use in men's wear.

Raglan shoulder pads

1/2"-thick, covered, raglan shoulder pads are used in jackets with set-in sleeves as well as in those with raglan sleeves (Figure 4.135). The 1/2" thickness is about the right amount of padding for most suit jackets. They work best when they're covered, because the covering allows the suiting fabric to

Figure 4.135

slide over the pad instead of sticking to it. The raglan style pad is longer than the traditional style, and it helps to support the sleeve cap area by adding shaping beyond the armscye seam, into the sleeve cap.

The raglan shoulder pad should be placed 1" or more down from the finished neck edge, and approximately 1" of the shaped end of the pad should extend into the sleeve cap. If you have small shoulders, just trim off the excess pad near the neck edge to make it smaller. Sew the shoulder pad to the jacket by hand, using a double strand of thread, and sewing the pad loosely to the shoulder seam allowances on both sides (Figure 4.136).

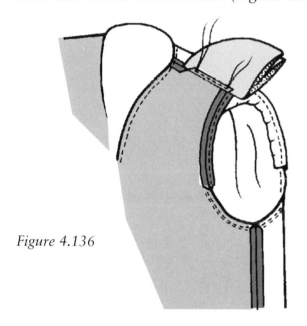

Figure 4.136

The ends of the raglan shoulder pad will float inside the jacket. Don't sew the shoulder pad in by machine, because that will compress the pad too much.

Set-in-sleeve shoulder pads
The traditional style of shoulder pad consists of cotton batting which is covered with

loosely-woven, muslin fabric on top and a non woven fabric on the bottom (Figure 4.137). The pad comes with or without a

Figure 4.137

layer of stiffener placed between the batting layers and the top covering. I prefer the pad with the stiffner. These shoulder pads are sewn in by hand to the seam allowances of the sleeve cap.

The shoulder pad should be 1" longer in the back of the jacket than the front, and the clip on the pad should be centered on the shoulder seam line. Fold the shoulder pad in half with the longest end of the pad 1" longer than the front end, and place a chalk mark to mark shoulder seam line if the pad is clipped in the wrong place.

Compare the shape of the sleeve end of the pad with the shape of the armscye by pinning the jacket front pattern piece to the back piece at the shoulder area. If the shape of the pad is not the same shape as the pattern, then mark with chalk to indicate where the pad needs to be trimmed. Remove the pattern pieces and trim off the excess shoulder pad following the markings.

Place the shoulder pad in the jacket lining up the thick end of the shoulder pad with the edge of the sleeve seam allowance. Pin the shoulder pad at the shoulder line only to hold it (Figure 4.138). Turn the jacket to the right side, and shape the shoulder pad over your

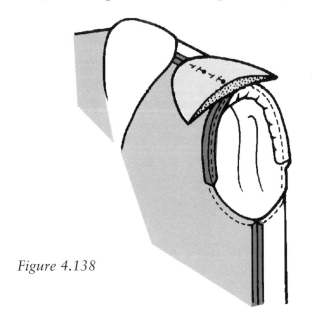

Figure 4.138

hand. Pin the pad from the right side at the armscye in several places to hold it in place (Figure 4.139). Turn to the wrong side and hand-stitch with stab stitches the pad to the seam allowances of the jacket and sleeve cap with double strands of thread (Figure 4.140).

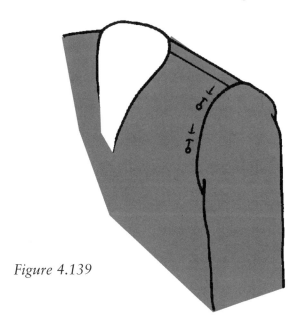

Figure 4.139

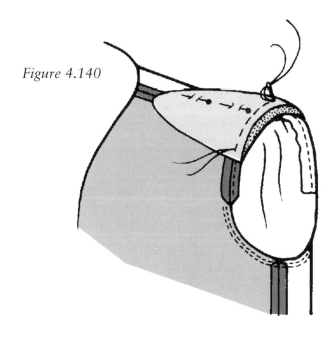

Figure 4.140

Making the body lining

Stay stitch the back neck edges of the lining pieces a scant 5/8" from the raw edge. Sew the center back seam, and press it flat. Sew the pleat about 1 1/2 in down (or wherever pattern calls for) at the top of the center back (Figure 4.141). If the pleat continues

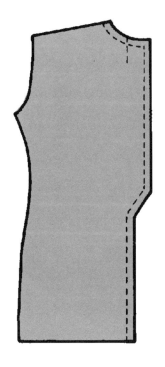

Figure 4.141

down to the hem allowance, sew it at the bottom of the center back (Figure 4.142). Press the pleat towards the right side of the

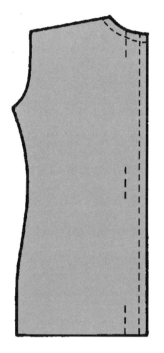

Figure 4.142

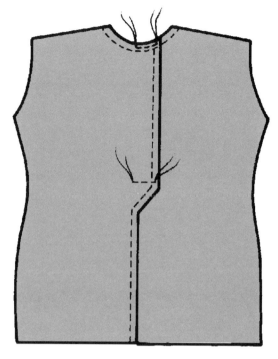

Figure 4.143

jacket from top to bottom, then sew across it at the neck edge, the waist line (Figure 4.143), and the hemline of the lining if the pleat extends the full length of the jacket (Figure 4.144).

If the jacket has side panels, sew the lining side panels to the lining front and back. Press the seam allowances flat, then open, clipping in shaped areas (I clip the lining seam allowances with pinking shears).

If the lining has darts, sew them in the lining front and back where indicated, and press flat. Then press the darts in the front toward the center front, and the darts in the back towards the center back. Clip the darts where needed to allow them to lay flat.

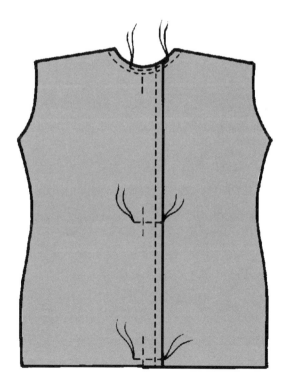

Figure 4.144

Sew the lining front to the lining back at the shoulder seams, and at the underarm seams or side panel seams, with right sides together. Press the seam allowances flat, then open, clipping in shaped areas.

Easing the lining sleeves

Sew the upper sleeve to the under sleeve at the longer seam allowance. Press the seam allowance flat, then open. To ease the lining sleeve caps as we did the jacket sleeve caps, use organza instead of wigan.

LINING THE JACKET

☛ *Tip: Organza is much stretchier than wigan, so don't stretch the organza strip too much or the sleeve cap will draw in far more than needed. If you don't have any organza on hand, you can use 1" wide "Seams Great" to shrink out the sleeve cap. When stretching "Seams Great," the curled edges should be facing out (towards you), not towards the fabric, so the sleeve cap will draw in as desired.*

Cut two strips of organza on the bias 15" long and 1" wide. Line up the edge of the bias fabric strip with the edge of the sleeve cap on the wrong side of the lining, starting at the notch in the front of the sleeve. Sew a few stitches to anchor the organza strip to the sleeve, sewing 1/2" from the raw edge. Stop with the needle down, raise the presser foot, and slightly stretch 2" to 3" of the organza strip and sew it down while holding it stretched. Repeat this process up to 1/2" before the top of the sleeve cap, stitch the

organza unstretched for 1" across the top of the sleeve cap, then start stretching and sewing the organza down to the notches on the back of the sleeve (Figure 4.145).

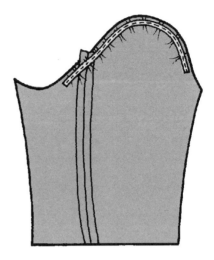

Figure 4.145

Sew the other seam allowance of the two piece sleeve. Press the seam allowance flat, then press open using a seam roll.

Setting in the lining sleeves

Pin the sleeve to the armscye, right sides together, lining up the notches and clips in the seam allowances, etc. If the sleeve cap is too small for the armscye in the area that was eased, release some of the tension by cutting through the organza strip and stitching line (Figure 4.146). You may have to do this in several places. If the sleeve cap requires more easing, pin in the ease as you pin the sleeve in place.

Begin sewing the sleeve cap into the armscye at the lower half of the armscye, sewing 5/8" from the raw edge, using a medium stitch length, and sewing with the sleeve cap next to the feed dog.

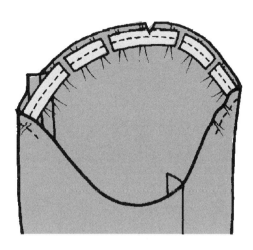

Figure 4.146

Sew a second row of stitches at the lower half of the armscye, next to the first stitching line to reinforce the armscye in this area. Trim the seam allowance next to the double stitching in the lower half to 1/4" (Figure 4.147). Place sleeve cap over a tailor's board, and press.

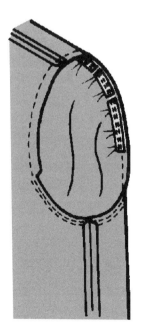

Figure 4.147

Inserting the lining

☞ *Important Tip: Always sew the lining to the facing with the facing next to the feed dog and the lining on top. Stop sewing every 3" with the needle down and raise the presser foot to allow the fabric to relax.*

First, clip the back neck edge of the lining to the stay stitching line with pinking shears. Starting at the center back, line up the seam allowances of the lining with the seam allowance of the back neck facing, right sides together, and pin them together. Line up the shoulder seam allowances of the lining and facing, and pin them together. Place additional pins to accurately line up the seam allowances around the curved area of the back neck facing.

Sew the lining to the facing with the back neck facing next to the feed dog and the lining on top, starting at the shoulder seam allowances and sewing to the center back. Repeat for the other half of the back neck facing (Figure 4.148).

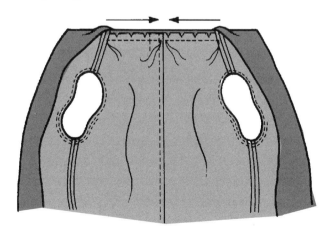

Figure 4.148

Pin the lining to the front facing, lining up notches. You'll probably have to ease in some of the lining at the bustline area; if so, distribute the ease as you pin. Leave 2" unpinned at the bottom of the lining. Start sewing at the shoulder seam allowances, stitching towards the bottom of the pinned lining, then repeat on the other side (Figure 4.149).

Figure 4.149

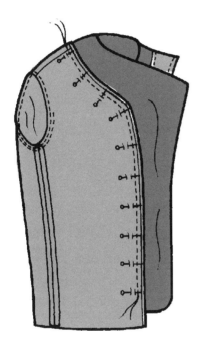

Check the lining to make sure there are no visible gathers or tucks along the seam. If you find any, rip the seam for several inches, distribute the excess, and re-stitch. Press the lining at the front and back neck facings.

Turn the sleeves of the jacket and lining to the wrong side, and line up the jacket-sleeve seam allowances with the lining-sleeve seam allowances, making sure you don't have the sleeves twisted. Machine baste with loosened tension or hand stitch the seam allowances

together starting about 3" down from the armscye, and stopping about 3" before the hem of the lining (Figure 4.150). The

Figure 4.150

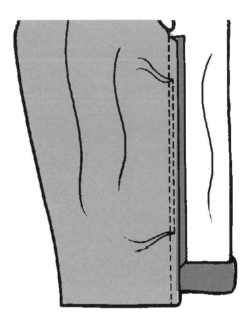

machine basting or hand sewing needs to be loose so the lining won't pull on the sleeve. If you have a two piece sleeve, repeat the proceedure with the other seam allowances.

Line up the side or side-back seam allowance of the jacket with the corresponding seam allowance of the lining, and machine baste or hand sew the seam allowances together loosely, starting and stopping about 3" from the ends, as with the sleeves.

Fold under 1/2" of the raw edge of the lining at the bottom. Place the folded lining edge against the hem allowance 1/2" down from the raw edge of the hem allowance and pin in place. Blind-hem the lining to the hem

allowance across the bottom of the jacket
(Figure 4.151). Hand sew the lining at each
corner where the lining joins the front facing
to finish.

Figure 4.151

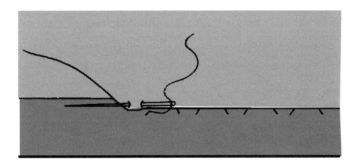

Turn the sleeves wrong side out, and blind-
hem the sleeve lining to sleeve hem allowance
by turning under 1/2" of the lining, and
placing the folded edge of the lining 1/2"
down from the raw edge of the sleeve hem.
Lightly press the lining, pressing in pleats at
the bottom of the jacket and sleeves. ◯

Chapter 5

Other Interfacing Options

Some tailors reinforce the fronts of women's and men's jackets with a combination of fusible interfacing and sew-in canvas chest pads instead of the all-fusible reinforcement I've described so far. This provides the best possible support from the shoulder to just above the bust, an area that often wrinkles on jackets worn by stooped or large-busted figures. The fusible interfacing required is more tightly woven than the commercial brands commonly found in fabric stores, and it's not usually available in the regular fabric stores (Sew Pro Workshop has made this interfacing available through the mail order; see page 6 for more information).

The canvas chest pads used in the upper chest portion of the jacket is a combination of tailor's canvas and lightweight polyester fleece. It's attached to the jacket at the lapel fold line, armscye and neck edge. You'll need 1 yd. of the 72" wide fusible interfacing (in place of the Armo Weft); 1/2 yd. of sew-in canvas; 1/2 yd. of sew-in polyester fleece; 1 yd. 3/4" cotton twill tape or 1 yd of 3/4" fusible straight tape; traditional shoulder pads with stiffner; and all other supplies listed on pages 1-3.

Fusible interfacing

Follow the instructions for preshrinking fusible interfacings given on page 8. Cut out the interfacing for the jacket front, the front side panel (if it has one), and the under collar. Don't include the hem allowance (Figure 5.1). Trim off 1/4" from the seam allowances, and fuse the interfacing onto suiting fabric (Figure 5.2).

Sew the side-front panel to the jacket front, right sides together, and press open the seam

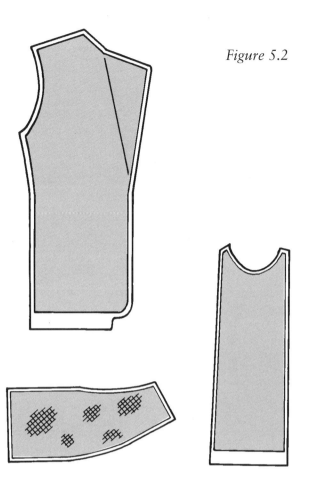

Figure 5.2

Figure 5.1

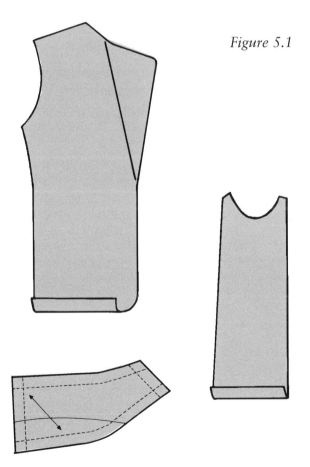

allowances, clipping where necessary. Follow the instructions given on pages 21-43 for sewing pockets, darts, and reinforcing the armscye. Draw the lapel fold line onto the jacket front, and follow the instructions given on pages 9-11 to measure the amount of ease to be taken in in this area.

Chest pads

◼ *Making the pattern*

To make a pattern for the chest pads, you'll need the pattern pieces for the jacket front, the front side panel (if it has one), and the jacket back. Lay these out on a large flat surface, and pin the jacket front pattern to the jacket back pattern at the shoulder seam line only. Pin the jacket front side panel to the jacket front at the armscye area (Figure 5.3).

Place a piece of pattern tissue or sew-in pellon on top of the pattern pieces and trace the edges of the armscye, the neck edge, and 3/8" back from the lapel fold line. Include the seam allowances of the neck edge and armscye. Draw a line from the neck edge at the shoulder area to the top portion of the

Figure 5.4

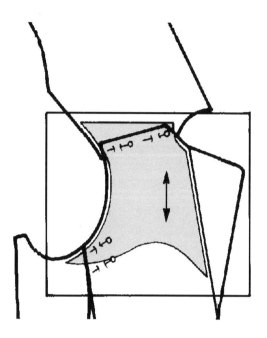

Figure 5.3

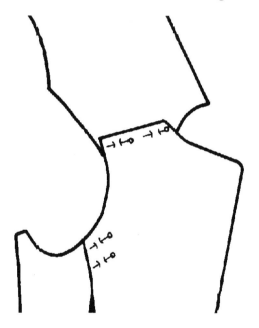

canvas chest piece (Figure 5.5). Pin it onto the canvas, on grain, and cut out. Cut out the polyester fleece from the same pattern piece, then trim off 1/4" from all edges of the fleece except for the armscye.

Figure 5.5

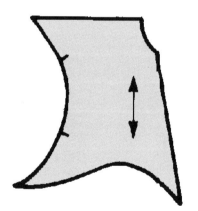

armscye of the jacket back, extending into the jacket back 1" to 1 1/2". Starting at the lower portion of the armscye, draw another line at an angle down to the lapel fold line, ending a few inches above the break of the lapel (Figure 5.4).

Trace the grain line from the jacket front onto the new pattern piece, draw in notches, etc., and cut it out. This is the pattern for the

■ *Constructing the chest piece*
Place the fleece on top of the canvas, lining up the armscye area first. The fleece should be smaller than the canvas at the lapel fold line, shoulder, and the lower portion of the

chest piece. Machine baste the fleece to the canvas using a long, loose zig-zag stitch, starting at the lapel fold line area and stitching across the bottom of the chest piece. Sew another row of zig-zag stitches next to the first row (Figure 5.6).

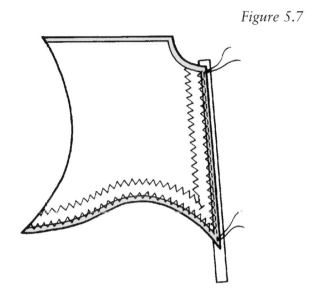

Figure 5.7

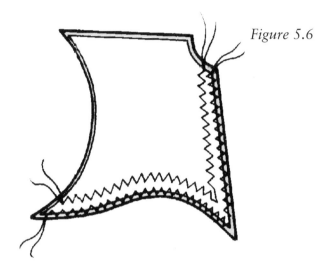

Figure 5.6

line, distributing the ease as you sew. With the pins still in, hand sew two more rows of stitches next to the first row to secure the twill tape (Figure 5.8). Press the eased area at the lapel fold line.

Cut a piece of 3/4" twill tape the length of the lapel fold line (including the seam allowance at the neck edge) down to the mark that indicates the end of the eased area. With the canvas on the bottom and the fleece uppermost, place 3/8" of the 3/4" twill tape on the lapel fold line edge of the chest piece and machine baste the twill tape to the canvas and fleece (Figure 5.7).

● Attaching the canvas to the jacket
Pin the chest piece to the jacket front with the canvas next to the suiting fabric, lining up the seam allowances of the armscye and neck edge. Pin the other 3/8" of the twill tape (with the chest piece attached) to the lapel fold line. Ease the lapel fold line into the twill tape, pinning in several places to hold, and hand sew to the jacket at the fold

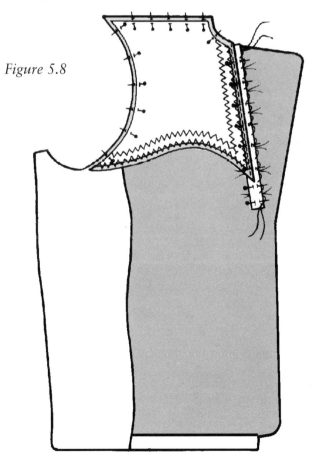

Figure 5.8

If you've chosen to use the fusible straight tape in place of the twill tape, machine baste the chest piece to the fusible straight tape with the glue side down, then pin it to the lapel fold line, easing as you pin. Press the fusible straight tape to the jacket at the lapel fold line, pressing in ease. Let the fabric cool before handling, then hand sew through the straight tape to secure the tape to the jacket (the tape can separate from the jacket if not secured). Hand a second row of stitches next to the first row.

● Securing the other edges
The canvas chest piece isn't attached to the jacket at the armscye and neck edge until after the sleeves and collar are sewn to the jacket. After the sleeves have been set into the jacket and the sleeve heads sewn in, attach the canvas and the fleece to the seam allowance of the armscye when sewing in the shoulder pads. The shoulder pads can be sandwiched between the layer of fleece and canvas. Pin them in place, and sew them to the seam allowance of the armscye and chest piece using stab stitches. The neck edge of the canvas can be loosely hand sewn to the seam allowance of the jacket after the collar has been attached. Follow the instructions in the previous section for finishing the suit jacket.

TAILORING WITH SEW-IN CANVAS

For the best-quality results, and when time is not an issue, use a sew-in canvas front interfacing. It's ideal for all fabrics except very lightweight ones such as thin silk. Top-quality designer jackets such as Escada and Burberrys are made with sew-in canvas fronts, and the prices (in 1993) for these jackets range from $900 to $1,300.

If you're sewing with a wool garbardine, I recommend that you use sew-in canvas interfacing because fusible interfacing doesn't always stay fused to gabardine. It may separate during dry cleaning. You may have had this experience already, when your jacket came back from the dry cleaners looking bubbled wherever interfacing was fused to the suiting fabric.

If you choose the all-sew-in method, you'll need: 1 1/2 to 2 yds of sew-in Acro or heavier weight canvas (for heavier fabrics) in place of Armo Weft; lightweight muslin fabric scraps; traditional style shoulder pads; and 2 yds of sleeve wigan.

Preparing the canvas
Pin the pattern pieces for the jacket front onto the canvas on grain and the under collar on the bias, and cut out. Transfer the front seam allowance, the under collar seam allowances, the lapel roll line, all darts and notches, the collar placement, etc., to the canvas pieces (Figure 5.9).

You can't include canvas in a seam allowance because it won't press flat, so next, cut off the seam allowance at the jacket front starting at the collar placement mark down to the bottom of the jacket front (Figure 5.10). You'll create a new seam allowance in this area by sewing muslin fabric strips to the canvas, as described below.

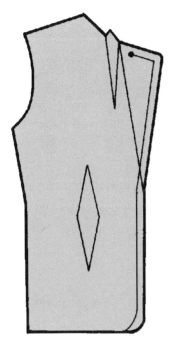

Figure 5.9

● Cutting the muslin strips
Pin the pattern piece for the jacket front on grain onto the lightweight muslin fabric. Cut around the pattern piece, starting at the lapel where the collar joins the lapel, cutting down to the bottom of the jacket front. Mark the

collar placement line and the break of the lapel. Remove the pattern piece, draw another line 1" from the cut edge of the jacket front onto the muslin fabric, and cut out the muslin on drawn line. Cut the muslin fabric strip in half at the mark for the break of the lapel (Figure 5.11).

Pin the muslin fabric strip for the upper half of the jacket to the top side of the canvas jacket front with 5/8" extending out from the canvas. Sew in place using a multiple zig-zag stitch, or two rows of straight stitching (Figure 5.12).

Figure 5.11

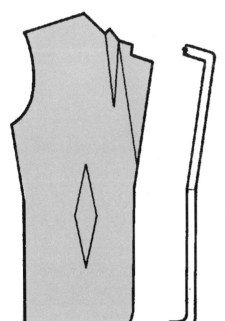

Figure 5.10

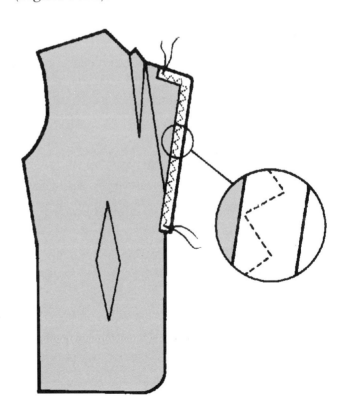

Pin the muslin fabric strip to the under side of the canvas for the lower half of the jacket with 5/8" of the muslin extending out from the canvas, and sew in place (Figure 5.13). Repeat the same proceedure for the other

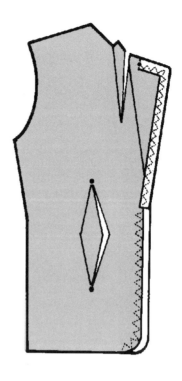

Figure 5.14

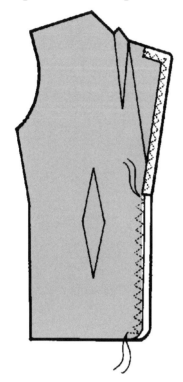

Figure 5.13

canvas front, keeping in mind that you are preparing the canvas for a right and left side of the jacket.

● Stitching darts in the canvas
The darts require special handling in canvas to eliminate bulk. Here are two ways to sew them together, after making sure the darts are clearly drawn on the canvas, including the little circles where the dart is suppose to meet.

Method One: Cut the dart from end to end along the line on one side (Figure 5.14). Pin the cut side of the dart on top of the uncut side, matching the cut edge to the line below, and sew the layers together with a multiple

zig-zag stitch (Figure 5.15). Trim away the excess canvas next to the stitching.

Method Two: Cut out the dart completely (Figure 5.16). Cut a strip of canvas the

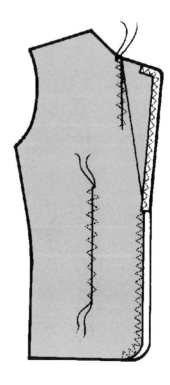

Figure 5.15

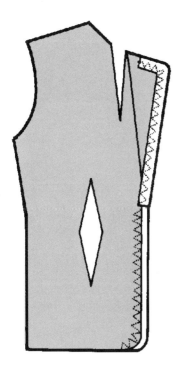

Figure 5.16

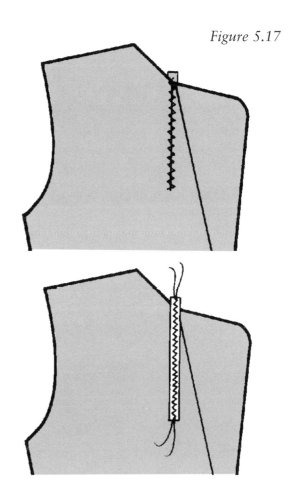

Figure 5.17

length of the dart, plus a couple of inches, and 1" wide. Butt the cut edges of the dart together, and pin to the fabric strip to hold everything in place. Sew the butt edges of the dart together to the fabric strip using a multiple zig-zag stitch. Trim off the excess fabric strip (Figure 5.17).

Method two is probably the better of the two methods described for sewing darts in canvas because the ends of the darts are more secure. If your jacket front is pieced, you can join the seam lines of the canvas by trimming one seam allowance away and overlapping the seam lines as in Method One.

● Padding the chest area
Here's how to reinforce the canvas at the chest area for maximum smoothness as done in men's wear. Follow the instructions for making a canvas chest pad on pages 75-77,

and sew it to the canvas at the lapel fold line and across the bottom of the chest pad area using a zig-zag stitch with the tension loosened (Figure 5.18).

Figure 5.18

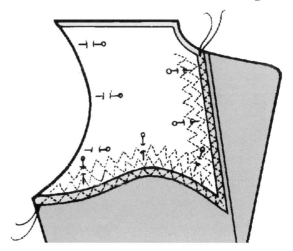

Preparing the jacket front

Follow the instructions given on pages 20-42 for stay-stitching the neck edge of the jacket front, reinforcing the armscye, and sewing in the pockets. Fuse a woven interfacing piece to the top of the lapel (if this interfacing becomes loose after dry cleaning, it won't affect the jacket because it is hidden under the lapel).

Attaching the canvas front to the jacket

Pin the canvas front to the jacket front, lining up the seam allowances. Hand baste the canvas to the jacket using long stitches, staying out of the armscye, the shoulder area, the neck edge, and the lapel (Figure 5.19).

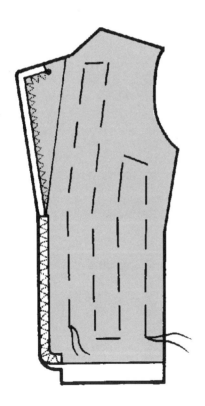

Figure 5.19

Pad stitch the lapel to the jacket starting at the lapel fold line, and working out to the edge of the lapel. As you stitch, build

shaping into the lapel by laying the lapel and canvas over your hand so they're rolling back from the jacket (Figure 5.20). It is not

Figure 5.20

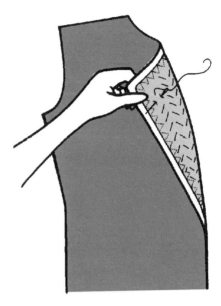

necessary to make either the stitches or the rows of the pad stitches any closer than about 3/4" apart. Do not pad stitch in the seam allowances.

Follow the instructions on pages 9-11 for taking in the ease at the lapel fold line using the twill tap, not the fusible straight tape. When sewing the twill tape to the fold line, make sure you are picking up a thread or two of the suiting fabric.

Follow the instructions on pages 43-45 for making the outside portion of the bound buttonholes, unless you are making machine buttonholes.

Attaching the jacket back to the front

Follow the instructions given on page 47-49 for preparing the jacket back, leaving out the fusible interfacing in the hem allowance. Instead, cut strips of bias wigan the width of the hem allowance and sew them to the edge of the hem allowance using a long stitch length.

Pin the jacket back to the jacket front at the shoulder seam allowance (do not include the canvas), and side seams. Sew the shoulder scams and side seams together, and press open clipping seam allowances where necessary.

Follow the instructions for preparing the sleeves, leaving out the fusible interfacing in the vent and hem allowances. Instead, pin the sleeve wigan to the bottom of the sleeve and baste in place, then follow all the other instructions for the mitred vent and sleeve buttons (Figure 5.21).

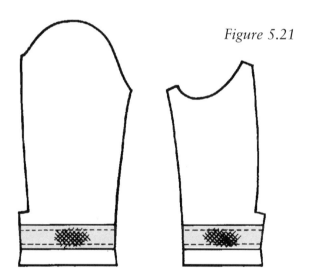

Figure 5.21

Follow the instructions for setting in the sleeves and putting in the sleeve heads, making sure you don't include the canvas (the canvas will be attached when the shoulder pads are sew in).

Preparing and attaching the under collar
Pin the under collar pieces together at the center back, sew, press the seam open, and trim the seam allowances to 1/4". Sew down the seam allowances, sewing close to the well of the seam. Fuse woven interfacing pieces to the ends of the collar (if these pieces should come loose during dry cleaning, it won't be seen) (Figure 5.22).

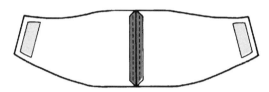

Figure 5.22

Trim the seam allowances (Figure 5.23). Pin the canvas to the under collar, and pad-stitch

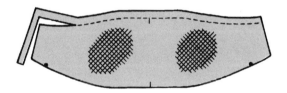

Figure 5.23

together using small pad stitches at the neck edge portion of the collar (Figure 5.24). Be sure you shape the collar as you pad stitch.

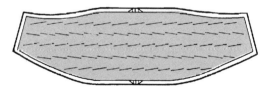

Figure 5.24

Pin the under collar to the jacket, and follow
the sewing instructions given on pages 50-51,
making sure that you don't include the
canvas. Press open the seam allowance.
Loosely hand-sew the neck edge of the
canvas to the neck edge to the jacket.

Finishing details

Follow the instructions on pages 51-53 to
sew the facing and upper collar to the jacket
(the facing and upper collar are not
interfaced). Finish the back of the bound
buttonholes as described on pages 56-57. Sew
in traditional-style shoulder pads as described
on page 67-68, when using chest pads. Insert
the lining in the same manner as described
on page 68-73. ◈

Index